Essays On

by

Oswald Mosley

Benito Mussolini

Alfredo Rocco &

Giovanni Gentile

Essays On Fascism

by

Oswald Mosley

Benito Mussolini

Alfredo Rocco &

Giovanni Gentile

ISBN-13: 978-1-913176-03-7

Sanctuary Press Ltd
71-75 Shelton Street
Covent Garden
London
WC2H 9JQ

www.sanctuarypress.com
Email: info@sanctuarypress.com

Contents

Oswald Mosley

Benito Mussolini

Alfredo Rocco

Giovanni Gentile

The Ideology of Fascism

by

Oswald Mosley

Oswald Mosley

The Ideology of Fascism
by Oswald Mosley

IDEAS in a void have never appealed to me; action must follow thought or political life is meaningless. The charge is sometimes made against me that my approach was at once too intellectual and too rough, too highbrow and too popular, a confusion between the study and the street. According to this theory I fell between two stools, and my leadership was consequently misconceived. It is a criticism which shows a misunderstanding of reality in modern politics. Anyone who cannot see the essential connection between thought and action as a concerted whole is unfit for the crude and yet subtle business of real politics in the twentieth century. It is not only necessary to have ideas but also to get them accepted and implemented. I have described the results of this attempt within the old parties, and have reached the point in this story where we went beyond their world in a direct appeal to the mass of the people. Then descended upon us the whole weight of the system in the organised smother, the denial of all means of expression and publicity; also the ineluctable force of organised violence, which sought to deprive us of our only remaining means of persuasion, the spoken word at the public meeting. In retrospect I put again the key question: what were we to do, go home and call it a day?

It is precisely at this point that intellect must finally decide whether to retire into the ivory tower or to enter the street with all that this entails. Intellect, to be effective, must now unite with will; otherwise the idea remains in the void. The 'thought-deed man' described in *The Alternative* was the need of the hour. It is not an attractive phrase, and I am not in love with it myself, but it expresses concisely the prime necessity of the modern world: men who can both think and act. So far from thought and action being antithetical—as the criticism of combining economic policies with the blackshirt movement suggested—they are essential complements in a creative whole; their union is indispensable, vital to a new birth.

In the light of contemporary experience this is undeniable.

Communism today commands half the world. It rests on a combination of Marxian thinking and communist party action. If the idea had just rested behind the whiskers would anything more have happened? It was in fact carried forward to the conquest of half the globe by the most brutal, ruthless and unscrupulous methods of action humanity has known; methods which, for reasons given, I believe will in the end be destructive of the idea, but certainly embodying action in extreme degree.

The superficial question may be raised whether the idea really had any relation to this kind of action, since not one in a hundred of Communist Party members understands Marxism, and not one in a million in the countries adhering to that creed has ever read Marx. Why then should this abstruse and far from popular doctrine have anything to do with the achievement at all? It is a superficial question, but it is difficult to answer without a psychological treatise which delves to the roots of human nature. In short reply, no movement of the human mind and spirit goes far unless it is inspired by an idea which, for better or worse, is a reality. It may be as obscure and contorted as Marxian economic theory or as clear and simple as the Christian doctrine of love, but it must be a reality in the sense that it appeals to some deep feeling in human nature.

When thought is obscure it must be translated into feeling to be effective. It is understood by an elite, and if it is a real and powerful idea it develops in them a certain attitude to life. This attitude is communicated to others who may not be familiar with the detail of the thinking, and it then becomes the feeling of the mass. A decisive idea thus transmuted into mass feeling can cause the birth of a new civilisation. Without such an idea, action is in the void, and without action the idea also rests in the void.

This truth has been well understood and applied in practical affairs by men who would appear the least likely to grasp it. For this reason, Stalin, amid all the brutalities of his actions, still tolerated and even encouraged the intellectuals, who must often have maddened him for much the same reasons which led Plato so unexpectedly to suggest the exclusion of poets from the Republic. Mao clearly felt the same necessity in encouraging both 'a hundred blooms' of the intellect and the development of the Red Guards. Lenin, who more than any other Russian communist leader, except possibly his close associate Trotsky, combined in himself the qualities of reflection and of action, undoubtedly recognised the same synthesis as a prerequisite of any movement of humanity to a new form, though it was less evident in his conduct during the turmoil of his period.

Fascism too derived much from its intellectual antecedents and by no means only from the relatively modern sources usually ascribed to it such as Sorel, Pareto, Proudhon, Nietzsche, and earlier English writers and men of action like Hobbes, Strafford, Bolingbroke, and later Carlyle. Some years ago Dr. Popper brought the industry and erudition of central Europe to London University and in his book, *The Open Society and its Enemies*, virtually denounced every outstanding thinker from Plato to Hegel as a fascist: I gladly accepted the gift, and expressed my appreciation for this confirmation of what I had long suspected.

Marxism was the negative of the nineteenth century, and yet communism required this intellectual background for any enduring success; more is needed than a bundle of grievances. A fortiori, the power of intellect and imagination will be necessary to the European creed which will be the positive of the twentieth century. During the long years since the war I have given my main energies to this necessity.

Time was too short for fascism to burgeon into a new culture which would later come to flower in a new civilisation. Indeed, the organic nature of fascism precluded a new culture in the sense of any sharp break with the past, because in essence it preserved and restored classic European values. I had already done the thinking which had produced a series of practical proposals to meet the immediate danger and long-term needs of my country; the urgency was then to implement them in practical action. It was not therefore just barbarism when at this stage I said that the men who can think are not enough, and I must go out to find the men who can feel, and do. It was recognition of a truth beyond the intellectuals with whom I was associated, and it deeply offended them precisely because it was beyond them. It is essential to surpass this antithesis of intellect and feeling in a synthesis which embraces both at a new level of thought and action.

When my original intellectual associates fell away in the shock of action which resisted organised violence, it was suggested that thereafter I was surrounded by stupid brutes who were conveniently classified as thugs. In fact, new intellectuals emerged from the study under the impact of those events, who at least equalled in mind and certainly surpassed in character those who had departed. In my company were some who would have added stature to any Cabinet and adorned any university. Their names were not well known because the smother was then operative to prevent their fame when they emerged, and threat to livelihood inhibited the open appearance of others. Our movement in these conditions became ever more like the iceberg with the main weight below the surface.

A recent book by John Harrison, *The Reactionaries,* apparently ascribed fascist tendencies to the following writers: Yeats, T. S. Eliot, Ezra Pound, Wyndham Lewis and D. H. Lawrence. In this case the title and the theme were a contradiction in terms, because writers cannot both be fascists and reactionaries. A movement of the Right has nothing to do with fascism, which can be described as revolutionary but not as reactionary.

The vilely libelled mass of our members were the very flower of the English people. They were men and women with the vision to see the doom coming to the values and position of their country and with the will and courage to resist it. Most of them were certainly men of feeling and of action rather than of the study, the type of the soldier rather than of the scholar, giving precedence to sword over gown, but it is such men who, in union with creative thinkers, build all movements of reality. In the rapid advance of our movement there was little time for academic sterilities, and even too little time, admittedly, for the serious discussion which is necessary to the advance of thought and development of policy. In that period time was always too short, and everything was too hurried; disabilities which subsequent experience repaired. I remember one of our best men, who after a spectacular R.A.F. career proved to have an extraordinary capacity for street leadership, saying to me: 'I have read little you have ever written because my work keeps me too busy, and I have heard little you have ever said, because at the meetings I am always looking round for the next Red who might have to go out, but—I feel with you'—and his regard was a tribute to the capacity for translating new thought and morality into feeling which can hold and inspire men with a dedicated passion. In the same way, I was always pleased beyond any other praise at the end of a speech when some fine old Englishman would come up to me and say: 'You have been saying what I felt all my life'. He meant that the speech had touched some deep chord in the eternal being of England.

This will no doubt be regarded as absurd by some who are called intellectuals and who possess every qualification for that title except

6

an intellect. Yet this is not sentiment, or worse; it is reality, the force which moves men. Leadership should be equally at home in the study of economics, in the homes of the poorest during moments of sorrow or happiness, in the merry scenes of English pubs and in the philosophic debates of universities. It must be interwoven with English and now with European life, both understanding and creative, both appreciative of the present and aspiring to new heights. Our action and also our thinking were continually developing. Even in the turmoil of pre-war politics fresh thought was added to the original economic concepts born within the Labour Party, but because fascism was so much a national creed, the new ideological development had little relation to contemporary thinking in the movements of the Continent.

Contrast has been the essence of my life, and it is good, provided it is expressed in two poles of an harmonious whole serving the same overriding purpose rather than in the discords of a split personality. I have given some account of the action in my fascist period which won the right to express at public meetings economic policies devised while I was still a member of the Labour Party. Now I must give some account of ideas in a quite different sphere of thought, which added ideology to the economics of my Labour Party days. These ideas seem to me crude and unsatisfactory in comparison with my thinking and writing since the Second World War and the enforced withdrawal into reading and reflection which it entailed for me. Nevertheless, it is difficult to contend in the light of my speech and writing in the thirties that fascism had no ideological background, though our English approach had not much to do with the main stream of fascist thought abroad. The derivation of this thinking is European, but it emphasises the English character of fascism in Britain because it is so remote from what fascist movements on the Continent were thinking or saying at that time, and in certain vital respects directly contradicted the continental approach to the same subjects.

My first speech with this theme was delivered in March 1933, at a choice of venue which in retrospect may seem curious—the English-Speaking Union, which was founded to promote Anglo-American friendship. After a conventional opening I said:

> 'Our opponents allege that fascism has no historic background or philosophy, and it is my task this afternoon to suggest that fascism has roots deep in history and has been sustained by some of the finest flights of the speculative mind.... So far it is to some extent true that the fascist philosophy has not assumed a very concrete and

definite form, but you must remember that the fascist faith has only been in existence little more than ten years: it is a growth of the last decade. Already, however, its philosophic background is capable of some formulation, and that has happened in a far shorter space of time than a corresponding development in any other great political faith of history. Just as the fascist movement itself, in several great countries, has advanced towards power at a phenomenal speed, so the fascist faith and philosophy as a permanent conception, an attitude to life, has advanced far more quickly than did the philosophies of the older faiths. Take liberalism: a very long interval elapsed between the writings of such men as Voltaire and Rousseau, and the final formation of the liberal creed in the hands of English statesmen at the end of the eighteenth and the beginning of the nineteenth century.

In fact, these great political movements and psychological upheavals only very slowly crystallised into a definite system of thought, as well as a system of action; and in the fascist case it is probably rather soon to expect at the end of ten years that it should have assumed a concrete, crystallised form.' This, of course, was true, and fascism then had only six years left before the turmoil of the Second World War which cut short its life.

It is clearly too much to hope that any doctrine born as an explosion of action in a time of national crisis can develop a complete philosophy in so short a space of time. The speech continued: 'Nevertheless, I believe that fascist philosophy can be expressed in intelligible terms, and while it makes an entirely novel contribution to the thought of this age, it can yet be shown to derive both its origin and its historic support from the established thought of the past. In the first instance, I suggest that most philosophies of action are derived from a synthesis of cultural conflicts in a previous period. Where, in an age of culture, of thought, of abstract speculation, you find two great cultures in sharp antithesis, you usually find, in the following age of action, some synthesis in practice between those two sharp antitheses which leads to a practical creed of action. This conception may seem to you to suggest, to some extent, a Spenglerian approach.'

Why in this context did I refer to a Spenglerian approach?—for the concept of two antitheses leading to a synthesis is clearly Hegelian; perhaps I thought that the spectre of Hegel would be too alarming for the English-Speaking Union. Goethe remarked that since Germans

8

found him so difficult, he must be impossible for foreigners. Referring to Spengler, I continued:

'It is quite true that the great German philosopher has probably done more than any other to paint in the broad background of fascist thought. Not very much more than that. And possibly he is inhibited from coming nearer to the subject by his innate pessimism, which, in its turn, I would humbly suggest to you arises from his entire ignorance of modern science and mechanical development. If you look through the Spenglerian spectacles, you are bound to come to a conclusion of extreme pessimism because they obscure the factor which for the first time places in the hands of man the ability entirely to eliminate the poverty problem. And I believe it is our German philosopher's misunderstanding of this immense new factor which leads him to his pessimistic conclusion. Nevertheless, that in no way invalidates his tremendous contribution to world thought.'

Before returning to Spengler and other concepts of philosophy I had some practical remarks to deliver on the fascist attitude to life:

'We demand from all our people an over-riding conception of public service. In his public life, a man must behave himself as a fit member of the State, in his every action he must conform to the welfare of the nation. On the other hand, he receives from the State in return, a complete liberty to live and to develop as an individual. And in our morality—and I think possibly I can claim that it is the only public morality in which private practice altogether coincides with public protestation—... the one single test of any moral question is whether it impedes or destroys in any way the power of the individual to serve the State. He must answer the questions: "Does this action injure the nation? Does it injure other members of the nation? Does it injure my own ability to serve the nation?" And if the answer is clear on all those questions, the individual has absolute liberty to do as he will; and that confers upon the individual by far the greatest measure of freedom under the State which any system ... or any religious authority has ever conferred.

'The fascist principle is private freedom and public service. That imposes upon us, in our public life, and in our attitude towards other men, a certain discipline and a certain restraint; but in our public life alone; and I should argue very strongly indeed that the only way to have private freedom was by a public organisation which brought some order out of the economic chaos which exists in the world today, and that such public organisation can only be secured by the methods of authority and of discipline which are inherent in fascism.

'Here we are brought at once into collision with the fundamental tenets of socialism and liberalism. Socialism differs, of course, sharply from liberalism in its conception of economic organisation; but in philosophy I think there are few socialists or liberals who would disagree that they really have a common origin if we go back far enough in the Voltaire-Rousseau attitude of life; and above all the latter. Rousseau, in our view, either made a big mistake, or was much misunderstood. Rousseau said: Equality. We reply, if you mean equality of opportunity, yes; if you mean equality of man, no. That is an absurdity. I believe personally that if he is properly read, Rousseau meant equality of opportunity.

'But that doctrine was seized upon by his later disciples as meaning the equality of man, that all men were equal. From that construction arises the whole fallacy, as we see it. It is a manifest and clear absurdity. One man, in mind and physique, differs immensely from another. It is not a question, as socialists often say, of moral or spiritual equality. That is a totally different thing. Morally and spiritually, the man who sweeps the floor of a big business may be vastly superior to the manager of that business. But the question is, which man is fitted to do which job. What is the proper function that he has to perform? Some people are good at one thing and some at another. Certainly we eliminate altogether the social class conception from fascism, because that rests upon the chance of heredity; but we do say that certain people are fitted by nature to do certain things, and others are not. And once you adopt that basis of thought, you challenge the whole conception of democracy.'

This must be one of the last occasions when I used the term democracy in what seems the perjorative sense, no doubt in reaction to the experience of government through which I had recently passed. It was my habit during only a brief period, for it soon seemed to me clear that democracy in its true sense —government of the people, by the people, for the people, as an expression of the natural, healthy will of the people when free from the deception of financial politics—was exactly what we wanted. It was the perversion of democracy and not democracy itself which we condemned; what I subsequently called financial democracy, and in my denunciation of the system I always used that phrase, arguing that the power of money within the prevailing system invariably prevented the fulfilment of the people's will which was the essence of true democracy. In this context I was aiming in particular at the replacement of the geographical by an occupational franchise, the vote according to occupation, craft or profession rather than according to residence; an informed vote. I still think it is a preferable system, but I no longer advocate it, as we have more urgent things to do, and with certain reforms the present system can be made to work effectively.

After establishing a case against chaotic egalitarianism, I argued in favour of complete equality of opportunity, the career open to talent: 'When a man has proved himself, he may rise to the greatest position in the land, and our whole educational system must be so devised'. Then came a return to Spengler and the main themes: my preoccupation with Caesarism in history and with science in the modern age. It was Spengler's profound understanding of Caesarism which first attracted me to him, but his appreciation of modern science was shallow, indeed scanty. The union of a Caesarian movement with science seemed to me at once the prime requirement of the modern age and the answer to the ultimate fatality predicted by Spengler.

First came an analysis of Caesarism in history and of the inevitable differences of form in the modern world: 'Now you may say, and say perhaps with some truth, that these doctrines have been heard before, that this was the basis of Bonapartism, or to go back still further to its origin, was the basis of Caesarism.

'It is, of course, true that fascism has an historic relation to Caesarism, but the modern world differs profoundly from the forms and conditions of the ancient world. Modern organisation is too vast and too complex to rest on any individual alone, however gifted. Modern Caesarism, like all things modern, is collective. The will and talent of the individual alone is replaced by the will and ability of the disciplined thousands who comprise a fascist movement. Every blackshirt is an individual cell of a collective Caesarism. The organised will of devoted masses, subject to a voluntary discipline, and inspired by the passionate ideal of national survival, replaces the will to power and a higher order of the individual superman. Nevertheless, this collective Caesarism, armed with the weapons of modern science, stands in the same historic relationship as ancient Caesarism to reaction on the one hand and to anarchy on the other. Caesarism stood against Spartacism on the one hand and the Patrician Senate on the other. That position is as old as the history of the last two thousand years. But they lacked, in those days, the opportunities for constructive achievement which are present today, and the only lesson that we can derive from the previous evidence of this doctrine is simply this; that whenever the world under the influence of Spartacus drifted to complete collapse and chaos, it was always what Spengler called the "fact-men" who extracted the world from the resultant chaos and gave mankind very often centuries of peace and of order in a new system and a new stability.

'It was done... by recognising certain fundamental facts of politics and of philosophy. Again, you have a certain wedding of two seemingly conflicting doctrines. We are often accused of taking something from the Right and something from the Left. Well, it is a very sensible thing to borrow from other faiths; to discard what is bad and keep what is good; and directly you get away from the old parliamentary mind, you of course see the wisdom of any such course. And fascism does, of course, take something from the Right and something from the Left, and to it adds new facts to meet the modern age. In this new synthesis of fascism, coming rather nearer to our immediate situation, we find that we take the great principle of stability supported by authority, by order, by discipline, which has been the attribute of the Right, and we marry it to the principle of progress, of dynamic change, which we take from the Left. Conservatism... believes in stability and supports it by its belief in order: but where Conservatism has always failed in the modern world is in its inability to perceive that stability can only be achieved through progress: that a stand-pat resistance to change precipitates the revolutionary situation which Conservatism most fears. On the other hand, the Left has always failed to realise, thanks to its Rousseau complex, that the only way to get progress is to adopt the executive instruments by which alone change is made possible.'

I was at this point weaving into fascist ideology my long-sustained synthesis of order and progress. '... You can only have stability if you are prepared to carry through orderly changes, because to remain stable you must adapt yourselves to the new facts of the new age. On the other hand, you can only have the progress which the Left desires if you adopt the executive instruments of progress.... 'Again you will say: "This is once more Caesarism or Bonapartism.... The basic principles remain the same; and, therefore, while your fascist movement may perform the purpose which Caesarism has performed before, may bring order out of chaos which the conflict between Spartacus and reaction has evoked, may for a few years or a few centuries give great peace to the world, it yet carries within itself its own decay, and does not really achieve what we believe to be necessary."

It was at this point that my thinking began to differ sharply from the attitude of the national socialist movement in Spengler's country of origin, for it appeared that intellectually the leaders saw the force of his argument but found no answer to it. Their propagandists felt that it was not an attractive doctrine to say to their members from the mass of the people: struggle, sacrifice and give your all to make a few men Caesars, to secure a last, glorious blossoming of a civilisation, and then eternal night. So they saluted Spengler in private, but silenced him in their public doctrine; pessimism and revolution are contradictions in terms. We, on the contrary, saw his thesis as the premise to the modern argument, and we summoned the mighty spirit of modern science to provide the answer. Caesarism and science together could evolve Faustian man; a civilisation which could renew its youth in a persisting dynamism, as I described it in my later writing. The speech continued:

'I believe the answer to that case, which is the only really valid case, is that always before the factor of modern science was lacking. You have now got a completely new factor. If you can introduce into your system of government a new efficiency—and everyone admits that such movements when they come to power are at least efficient: if you can bring to government for even a few years an executive power and an efficiency which gets things done, you can release ... the imprisoned genius of science to perform the task which it has to perform in the modern world. Whatever our divergent views on the structure of the State and economics may be, I think we must all agree that it would be possible, by sane organisation of the world, with the power of modern science and of industry to produce, to solve once and for all the poverty problem, and to abolish... the worst attributes of disease and suffering from the world. Therefore, if it is possible to have an efficient form of government, you have available for such a system, for the first time in history, an instrument by which the face of the earth might be changed for all time.

Once the essential has been done, once modern science and technique have been released and have performed their task, once you have changed your political and philosophic system from a transitory and political to a permanent and technical basis, there will be no more need of the politics and of the controversies which distract the world today. The problem of poverty will be solved, the major problems will be banished, as they can be, and as everybody knows they can be, if modern science is properly mobilised. Then mankind will be liberated for the things in life which really matter.

'Therefore, while it is perhaps true that certain of these phenomena in the eternal recurrences of history have been seen in the world before, and seen with great benefit to mankind, yet never before have the great executive movements possessed the opportunity to complete their task which modern science and invention now confer upon them.

'At a moment of great world crisis, a crisis which in the end will inevitably deepen, a movement emerges from a historic background which makes its emergence inevitable, carrying certain traditional attributes derived from a very glorious past, but facing the facts of today armed with the instruments which only this age has ever conferred upon mankind. By this new and wonderful coincidence of instrument and of event the problems of this age can be overcome, and the future can be assured in a progressive stability. Possibly this is the last great world wave of the immortal, the eternally recurring Caesarian movement; but with the aid of science, and with the inspiration of the modern mind, this wave shall carry humanity to the farther shore.

'Then, at long last, Caesarism, the mightiest emanation of the human spirit in high endeavour toward enduring achievement, will have performed its world mission in the struggle of the ages, and will have fulfilled its historic destiny. A humanity released from poverty and from many of the horrors and afflictions of disease to the enjoyment of a world re-born through science, will still need a fascist movement transformed to the purpose of a new and nobler order of mankind; but you will need no more the strange and disturbing men who in days of struggle and of danger and in nights of darkness and of labour, have forged the instrument of steel by which the world shall pass to higher things.'

In retrospect, I see at this point the merit of this speech: the union of Caesarism and modern science which could be the decisive fact of history, a final union of will with thought in a limitless achievement.

After this lapse of time it still seems to me a very considerable thesis— now reinforced by the subsequent development of science—that for the first time executive men could find the means to do something truly great and enduring. The union of a revolutionary movement, which is a modern Caesarism, with the force of modern science could be nothing less than this. The genius of science imprisoned by the dull mediocrity of politics which could not realise its potential would be released for a world transforming task. The new men of politics in relation to science would transcend even the relationship of the men of the renaissance to art and a new world could be born of this union.

The speech in conclusion expressed the belief that fascism itself would eventually pass to make way for a higher order of mankind. Beyond the 'fact men' of Caesarism could already be discerned 'a new form, shadowy, as yet obscure, visible in outline only, but still a higher form' (as I wrote later) 'the will to power and the will to beauty in the mystical union which is all achieving'.

It is, of course, possible to comment on the speech of 1933 that all this was just a diffuse and romantic way of saying: if you bring together executive men with modern science in an efficient system of government, you will get things done. In the present day I have some intellectual sympathy with the contemporary preference for short, flat, clear statement, but the method belongs to this humdrum period when action is not yet generally felt to be essential. If you want to move men to do great things in a great way, you must set plain facts in the perspective of history and illumine them with a sense of destiny.

I returned to some of the same themes five years later in *Tomorrow We Live*; in the last chapter I described briefly the situation of Britain as I saw it in relation to other civilisations which had succumbed to the forces now threatening us:

'British Union emerges from the welter of parties and the chaos of the system to meet an emergency no less menacing than 1914, because it is not so sudden or so universally apparent. British Union summons our people to no less an effort in no less a spirit. Gone in the demand of that hour was the clamour of faction, and the strife of section, that a great nation might unite to win salvation. A brotherhood of the British was born that in the strength of union was invincible and irresistible. Today the nation faces a foe more dangerous because he dwells within, and a situation no less grave because to all it is not yet visible. We have been divided, and we have been conquered, because by division of the British alone we can be conquered. Class against class, faction against faction, party against party, interest against interest, man against man, and brother against brother has been the tactic of the warfare by which the British in the modern age, for the first time in their history, have been subdued. We have been defeated, too, at a moment in our history when the world was at our feet, because the heritage won for us by the heroism of our fathers affords to the genius of modern science and the new and unprecedented triumph of the human mind an opportunity of material achievement leading, through the gift of economic freedom, to a higher spiritual civilisation than mankind, in the long story of the human race, has yet witnessed.

Can we recapture the union of 1914 and that rapturous dedication of the individual to a cause that transcends self and faction, or are we doomed to go down with the Empires of history in the chaos of usury and sectional greed? That is the question of the hour for which every factor and symptom of the current situation presses decision. Is it now possible by a supreme effort of the British spirit and the human will to arrest what, in the light of all past history, would appear to be the course of destiny itself? For we have reached the period, by every indication available to the intellect, at which each civilisation and Empire of the past has begun to traverse that downward path to the dust and ashes from which their glory never returned. Every fatal symptom of the past is present in the modern situation, from the uprooting of the people's contact with the soil to the development of usury and the rule of money power, accompanied by social decadence and vice that flaunts in the face of civilisation the doctrine of defeat and decline.'

These tendencies in contemporary life, which were the subject of daily comment in our speeches at mass public meetings and were the theme of our policies seeking to reverse them, were interrupted by the war; the British showed that they were indeed still capable of the effort I had asked them to make, though for very different purposes. But a revival of the national will for the brief period of war is not enough, and the evils we combated in the thirties have now returned with renewed force in a general situation of national weakness much aggravated by war. This analysis brought me in the conclusion of this book inevitably to Spengler:

'Above the European scene towers in menace Spengler's colossal contribution to modern thought, which taught our new generation that a limit is set to the course of civilisations and Empires, and that the course that once is run is for ever closed. Every indication of decadence and decline which he observed as a precursor of the downfall of a civilisation is apparent in the scene, and from all history he deduced the sombre conclusion that the effort of "Faustian" man to renew his youth, and to recapture the dawn of a civilisation, must ever fail. History is on the side of the great philosopher, and every sign of the period with fatal recurrence supports his view. His massive pessimism, supported by impressive armoury of fact, rises in challenge and in menace to our generation and our age. We take up that challenge with the radiant optimism born of man's achievements in the new realm of science, that the philosopher understood less well than history, and born, above all, of our undying belief in the invincible spirit of that final product of the ages—the modern man. We salute our great antagonist, from whose great warning we have learnt so much, but we reject utterly the fatality of his conclusion. We believe that modern man, with the new genius of modern science within him and the inspiration of the modern spirit to guide him, can find the answer to the historic fatality.'

Before returning to the theme of Spengler I summarised two objects of our continual attack, which were only related to Spengler in that he too was determinist in attitude. There were really three doctrines of determinism at that time, Marx, Freud and Spengler; all in some aspects rejected by our belief in a Faustian revival of the human will. Spengler at least recognised the possibility of a temporary reply to his own determinism—'. . . when money is celebrating its last victories, . . . and the Caesarism that is to succeed approaches with calm, firm tread . . .'—while I went further and affirmed that with the aid of modern techniques a final answer could find permanent expression in a 'persisting dynamism'.

I referred to the determinism of Marx and Freud: 'The doctrines of modern disintegration are classic in form, and pervade the political parties, which fade from a flaccid and universal "liberalism" into the sheer disruption and corruption of socialism serving usury. The doctrinaires of the immediate past come to the aid of political defeatism with the negation of manhood and self-will, and the scientific formulation of surrender as a faith. In the sphere of economics Marx portrays humanity as the helpless victim of material circumstance, and in the sphere of psychology Freud assists the doctrine of human defeatism with the teaching that self-will and self-help are no longer of any avail, and that man is equally the helpless toy of childish and even pre-natal influence. Marx's "materialist conception of history" tells us that man has been moved by no higher instinct than the urge of his stomach, and Freud supports this teaching of man's spiritual futility with the lesson that man can never escape from the squalid misadventures of childhood. . . . This predestination of materialism has proved in practice even more destructive of the human will and spirit than the old and discredited "predestination of the soul". It has paralysed the intellectual world into the acceptance of surrender to circumstance as an article of faith.

'To these destructive doctrines of material defeatism our renaissant creed returns a determined answer. To Marx we say it is true that if we observe the motive of a donkey in jumping a ditch, we may discern a desire to consume a particularly luxuriant thistle that grows on the other side. On the other hand, if we observe a man jumping a ditch, we may legitimately conclude that he possesses a different and possibly a higher motive. To Freud we reply that, if indeed man has no determination of his own will beyond the idle chances of childhood, then every escape from heredity and environment, not only of genius but of every determined spirit in history, is but a figment of historic imagination. In answer to the fatalistic defeatism of the "intellectual" world our creed summons not only the whole of history as a witness to the power and motive force of the human spirit, but every evidence and tendency of recent science.'

Some of my contemporaries were excessively preoccupied with Marx and Freud, John Strachey particularly so, and I remember teasing him with the observation: 'You are governed above the waist by Marx, below the waist by Freud, but no part of you by Strachey'; he was a good-humoured fellow. Some of these references to Marx and Freud — who at least were serious people worthy of serious study — have something of the flippancy of Disraeli's intervention in the Darwinian controversy at Oxford: 'The question is whether man is descended from angel or ape; I am on the side of the angels'. I should have more now to say on these subjects, but truth is not necessarily lacking from pithy expression.

At the end of *Tomorrow We Live* I returned to the answer politics and science could together give to the doom which threatened yet another civilisation:

'So man emerges for the final struggle of the ages, the supreme and conscious master of his fate, to surmount the destiny that has reduced former civilisations to oblivion. He advances to the final ordeal armed with weapons of the modern mind that were lacking to any previous generation in the crisis of a civilisation. The wonders of our new science afford him not only the means with which to conquer material environment, in the ability to wrest wealth in abundance from nature, but in the final unfolding of the scientific revelation probably also the means of controlling even the physical rhythm of a civilisation. Man for the first time carries to the crisis of his fate weapons with which he may conquer even destiny. But one compelling necessity remains, that he shall win within himself the will to struggle and to conquer. Our creed and our movement instil in man the heroic attitude to life, because he needs heroism. Our new Britons require the virility of the Elizabethan combined with the intellect and method of the modern technician. The age demands the radiance of the dawn to infuse the wonder of maturity. We need heroism not just for war, which is a mere stupidity, but heroism to sustain us through man's sublime attempt to wrestle with nature and to strive with destiny.'

This way of writing is very different from the flat statements of contemporary fashion by writers whose only discernible ambition is to make the world as dull as themselves, precisely because it aimed at expressing the inspiration of men with a dynamic purpose who were determined to play a decisive part at a turning-point in history; style can reflect both vitality and fatigue, and I prefer the former if it retains clarity. "What really interested me in Spengler was his realisation that at certain points in history the fact-men, supported by popular but realistic movements, always emerged to arrest the decline of a civilisation. This aspect of Caesarism had fascinated me long before I read Spengler, and the possibilities of modern science had equally engaged me over a long period. It seemed clear to me that this conjunction was the instrument which had never before been available to the architects of state, and it could give the new fact-men at last the means to build a civilisation which could endure when they and their revolutionary impulse had passed. The modern age therefore presented a possibility which the world had never known before, and this could transmute the massive pessimism of Spengler's theory into an enduring and achieving optimism.

Spengler also gave new impulses to my thinking because he accentuated the sense of impending disaster if effective action were not taken. His theory was foreign to Britain and rejected by German government for reasons already described. His approach to history later became familiar to the British in the outstanding contribution of Arnold Toynbee, who acknowledged his debt to Spengler but added much in his 'challenge and response' theory with the picture of civilisations which had achieved renaissance by vigorous responses to the challenge of disaster, even without the aid of modern science. For my purpose this reinforced the view that the doom of our civilisation — a looming menace not only in economics but in national psychology, as it seemed to me — could be met and overcome by the will of a determined movement to national renaissance. Finally, Toynbee appeared to me, like Spengler, to drift from his challenging and indeed inspiring premises to another but almost equally lame conclusion; nevertheless, his contributions both to history and to the possible revival of the human spirit were important.

Six months after my speech to the English-Speaking Union, in the autumn of 1933, I met a remarkable man who then joined the party and became one of my most valuable colleagues. This was Raven Thomson, who in 1932 had published a book of exceptional interest on Spengler which I read when we came together. His approach differed from mine because his conclusion was as pessimistic as Spengler's, and his concept of the immediate future seemed to me an almost ant-heap collectivism. I had said in my E.S.U. speech that modern Caesarism would inevitably have a collective character, but his collective ideas seemed to go much too far in eliminating individual influence. The reason certainly was that at the time he wrote the book he was a communist. When he joined our movement we had many discussions and his collectivism began to admit a considerable place for individual influence, while his pessimism gradually changed to the most determined optimism I have ever encountered. Whether this metamorphosis was due to his contact with me, or to a blow he received on the head from a brick at one of his first appearances as a speaker for the party was often the subject of genial enquiry when he first appeared in a black shirt at the bar of the spacious 'barracks' which we acquired about that time in King's Road.

This exceptional thinker emerged from the study at the age of nearly forty to become a man of action and one of the finest fighters for our cause we ever knew. Intellectually Raven Thomson towered above the men I had known in the Labour Cabinet of 1929, and in firmness of character he seemed in an altogether different category to most of the contemporary politicians. Despite his academic background, he developed an exuberant enthusiasm for the work of the party and became one of its most effective speakers, as well as an outstanding writer. For years he edited the party paper, and was more than a match in controversy for the few challengers he encountered from the other side. Yet this honest man and devoted patriot, together with his companions of the blackshirt, was subjected to every insult in the catalogue of calumny which begins with the word 'thug'. This abuse, as vile as it was silly, came from every corner-boy of the intellect simply because he was associated with me in an effort of national renaissance. His offence was that he dared to choose that hard path in preference to his previous happy life, in the seclusion of his library and the company of his family. He died young, and we his friends will always feel that the prison years and the decline of his country combined to curtail a life which would have been of brilliant service to the nation. His colleague, Neil Francis-Hawkins, our chief organiser before the war, a man of outstanding character and ability, also died young for similar reasons. I shall mention no other blackshirts by name because this would be invidious among so many splendid men and women ; these two may rest as the monument of those who died and the inspiration of those who live.

The Corporate State is scarcely an appropriate subject for inclusion in an ideological study of fascism because it is essentially a system for the economic organisation, but it contains a concept of the state which enters the sphere of ideology. The original corporate thinking belongs to Mussolini, and in England its chief protagonist was Raven Thomson. My own effort was then on the lines of my thinking in the Birmingham proposals and in my resignation speech, which seemed to me to offer a more direct and thorough solution of the prevailing economic problems. Throughout my subsequent life my ideas evolved much more in the direction suggested by that thinking than in the tradition of the Corporate State.

What attracted me in the ideological aspect of the Corporate State was a government strong enough to keep the ring for the producer and to protect the interests of the consumer. Just as the centralised authority of the Tudor kings protected the citizens from the depredations of the robber barons, who had previously held all private life and enterprise up to ransom, so at this stage of society would the corporate system protect and promote a genuine private enterprise in face of the large industrial combines and concentrations of financial power. In The Greater Britain (1932), I wrote that government or the corporate system would 'lay down the limits within which individuals and interests may operate. Those limits are the welfare of the nation—not, when all is said, a very unreasonable criterion. Within these limits, all activity is encouraged; individual enterprise and the making of profit are not only permitted but encouraged, so long as that enterprise enriches rather than damages by its activity the nation as a whole.'

Defining the Corporate State I wrote: 'In psychology it is based on teamwork; in organisation it is the rationalised State. ... It is this machinery of central direction which the Corporate State is designed to supply ... it envisages, as its name implies, a nation organised as the human body. Every part fulfils its function as a member of the whole, performing its separate task, and yet, by performing it, contributing to the welfare of the whole. The whole body is generally directed by the central driving brain of government without which no body and system of society can operate.'

I related the corporate machinery suggested to my previous ideas in government and to other English thinking: 'The idea of a National Council was, I believe, first advanced in my speech of resignation from the Labour Government in May 1930. The idea has since been developed by Sir Arthur Salter [a distinguished Civil Servant, at one time head of the Civil Service] and other writers. A body of this kind stands or falls by the effectiveness of the underlying organisation. It must not consist of casual delegates from unconnected bodies, meeting occasionally for *ad hoc* consultation. The machinery must be permanently functioning and interwoven with the whole industrial and commercial fabric of the nation.'

There are many ideas of the corporate system which can make valuable contribution to the present situation. For instance, some of the policies of Mussolini's Corporate State were in certain respects practically indistinguishable from co-partnership, which had previously been advocated in England by Lord Robert Cecil and myself, and in recent times has been rediscovered by the young Liberals. Quaint indeed are the divergencies caused by muddled thinking and obscure terminology in the course of controversial politics.

My criticism of the corporate system in the light of experience and further thought is that it was too bureaucratic and insufficiently dynamic; in fact, I felt this at the time, as the different form of my writings shows. The elaborate organisation could maintain equilibrium, but did not secure sufficiently the progress which is not only humanly desirable but essential in a world driven forward by science. I wrote in The Greater Britain that 'industrial organisations will certainly not be confined merely to the settlement of questions of wages and of hours. They will be called upon to assist, by regular consultation, in the general economic policy of the nation.' Yet the idea of organisation was over-emphasised and the direction of organisation was insufficiently considered, and this was my view of the Italian concept as well as the writings of Raven Thomson, as I told him at the time.

It is at this point that I consider my post-war thinking concerning the wage-price mechanism far surpasses my thinking within the Labour Party and also within the fascist movement. The concept of the wage-price mechanism is less bureaucratic and more dynamic; with far less detailed interference, it maintains a continuous momentum in the achievement of the ever-higher standards of life which are essential to absorb the production of modern science. It has the conscious direction and defined objectives which the Corporate State to a large extent lacked. Therefore in my opinion the wage-price mechanism surpasses the Corporate State in economics as effectively as the doctrine of higher forms transcends my thinking of the thirties in the ideological sphere.

Two valuable ideas remain from the corporate period. The first is the State strong enough to keep the ring for producer and consumer in face of the large combinations of industrial and financial power; also - always inherent in my thinking - not only strong enough to hold the ring for science, but wise enough to make the support of science a first priority of the State. The second is the State regarded as an organic being which represents the past, the present and the future of a civilisation, an entity which asks the individual to recognise what he owes to those who preceded him and to posterity; an idea of the State as trustee for the whole course of a people and not merely as the servant of transient whim and fashion which may destroy what sacrifice and heroism have created.

Thus we return to the determination to achieve national renaissance in the thirties, rising in phoenix form from the flames of the explosion against conditions humanly intolerable and scientifically unnecessary, which seemed to us an expression of brutality and stupidity. Men and women simply felt that Britain had been great and should be great again, greater still. We owed it to the country we loved and to the mind, will and spirit of the English which derived from three thousand years of European history. I tried at the end of The Greater Britain to express this dedication in language combining the real and the ideal:

'In a situation of so many and such diverse contingencies nobody can dogmatise upon the future. We cannot say with certainty when catastrophe will come, nor whether it will take the form of a sharp crisis or of a steady decline to the status of a second-rate power. All that we can say with certainty is that Britain cannot muddle on much longer without catastrophe, or the loss of her position in the world. Against either contingency it is our duty to arouse the nation. To meet either the normal situation of political action, or the abnormal situation of catastrophe, it is our duty to organise. Therefore, while the principles for which we fight can be clearly described in a comprehensive system of politics, of economics and of life, it would be folly to describe precisely in advance the road by which we shall attain them. A great man of action once observed: "No man goes very far who knows exactly where he is going", and the same observation applies with some force to modern movements of reality in the changing situations of today

'We ask those who join us to march with us in a great and hazardous adventure. We ask them to be prepared to sacrifice all, but to do so for no small and unworthy ends. We ask them to dedicate their lives to building in this country a movement of the modern age, which by its British expression shall transcend, as often before in our history, every precursor of the Continent in conception and in constructive achievement.

'We ask them to re-write the greatest pages of British history by finding for the spirit of their age its highest mission in these islands. Neither to our friends nor to the country do we make any promises; not without struggle and ordeal will the future be won. Those who march with us will certainly face abuse, misunderstanding, bitter animosity, and possibly the ferocity of struggle and of danger. In return, we can only offer to them the deep belief that they are fighting that a great land may live.'

The Doctrine of Fascism
by Benito Mussolini

Fundamental Ideas.

1. Philosophic Conception.

Like every concrete political conception, Fascism is thought and action. It is action with an inherent doctrine which, arising out of a given system of historic forces, is inserted in it and works on it from within. It has therefore a form correlated to the contingencies of time and place; but it has at the same time an ideal content which elevates it into a formula of truth in the higher region of the history of thought.

There is no way of exercising a spiritual influence on the things of the world by means of a human will-power commanding the wills of others, without first having a clear conception of the particular and transient reality on which the will-power must act, and without also having a clear conception of the universal and permanent reality in which the particular and transient reality has its life and being. To know men we must have a knowledge of man; and to have a knowledge of man we must know the reality of things and their laws. There can be no conception of a State which is not fundamentally a conception of Life. It is a philosophy or intuition, a system of ideas which evolves itself into a system of logical contraction, or which concentrates itself in a vision or in a faith, but which is always, at least virtually, an organic conception of the world.

2. Spiritualized Conception.

Fascism would therefore not be understood in many of its manifestations (as, for example, in its organizations of the Party, its system of education, its discipline) were it not considered in the light of its general view of life. A spiritualized view.

Benito Mussolini

The Doctrine of Fascism

To Fascism the world is not this material world which appears on the surface, in which man is an individual separated from all other men, standing by himself and subject to a natural law which instinctively impels him to lead a life of momentary and egoistic pleasure. In Fascism man is an individual who is the nation and the country. He is this by a moral law which embraces and binds together individuals and generations in an established tradition and mission, a moral law which suppresses the instinct to lead a life confined to a brief cycle of pleasure in order, instead, to replace it within the orbit of duty in a superior conception of life, free from the limits of time and space a life in which the individual by self-abnegation and by the sacrifice of his particular interests, even by death, realizes the entirely spiritual existence in which his value as a man consists.

3. Positive Conception of Life as a Struggle.

It is therefore a spiritual conception, itself also a result of the general reaction of the Century against the languid and materialistic positivism of the Eighteenth Century. Anti-positivist, but positive: neither sceptical nor agnostic, neither pessimistic nor passively optimistic, as are in general the doctrines (all of them negative) which place the centre of life outside of man, who by his free will can and should create his own world for himself.

Fascism wants a man to be active and to be absorbed in action with all his energies; it wants him to have a manly consciousness of the difficulties that exist and to be ready to face them. It conceives life as a struggle, thinking that it is the duty of man to conquer that life which is really worthy of him: creating in the first place within himself the (physical, moral, intellectual) instrument with which to build it.

As for the individual, so for the nation, so for mankind. Hence the high value of culture in all its forms (art, religion, science) and the supreme importance of education. Hence also the essential value of labour, with which man conquers nature and creates the human world (economic, political, moral, intellectual).

4. Ethical Conception.

This positive conception of life is evidently an ethical conception. And it comprises the whole reality as well as the human activity which domineers it. No action is to be removed from the moral sense; nothing is to be in the world that is divested of the importance which belongs to it in respect of moral aims. Life, therefore, as the Fascist conceives it, is serious, austere, religious; entirely balanced in a world sustained by the moral and responsible forces of the spirit. The Fascist disdains the "easy" life.

5. Religious Conception.

Fascism is a religious conception in which man is considered to be in the powerful grip of a superior law, with an objective will which transcends the particular individual and elevates him into a fully conscious member of a spiritual society. Anyone who has stopped short at the mere consideration of opportunism in the religious policy of the Fascist Regime, has failed to understand that Fascism, besides being a system of government, is also a system of thought.

6. Historical and Realist Conception.

Fascism is an historical conception in which man could not be what he is without being a factor in the spiritual process to which he contributes, either in the family sphere or in the social sphere, in the nation or in history in general to which all nations contribute. Hence is derived the great importance of tradition in the records, language, customs and rules of human society. Man without a part in history is nothing.

For this reason Fascism is opposed to all the abstractions of an individualistic character based upon materialism typical of the Eighteenth Century; and it is opposed to all the Jacobin innovations and utopias. It does not believe in the possibility of "happiness" on earth as conceived by the literature of the economists of the Seventeenth Century; it therefore spurns all the teleological conceptions of final causes through which, at a given period of history, a final systematization of the human race would take place. Such theories only mean placing oneself outside real history and life, which is a continual ebb and flow and process of realizations.

Politically speaking, Fascism aims at being a realistic doctrine; in its practice it aspired to solve only the problems which present themselves of their own accord in the process of history, and which of themselves find or suggest their own solution. To have the effect of action among men, it is necessary to enter into the process of reality and to master the forces actually at work.

7. The Individual and Liberty.

Anti-individualistic, the Fascist conception is for the State; it is for the individual only in so far as he coincides with the State, universal consciousness and will of man in his historic existence. It is opposed to the classic Liberalism which arose out of the need of reaction against absolutism, and had accomplished its mission in history when the State itself had become transformed in the popular will and consciousness.

Liberalism denied the State in the interests of the particular individual; Fascism reaffirms the State as the only true expression of the individual.

And if liberty is to be the attribute of the real man, and not of the scarecrow invented by the individualistic Liberalism, then Fascism is for liberty. It is for the only kind of liberty that is serious—the liberty of the State and of the individual in the State. Because, for the Fascist, all is comprised in the State and nothing spiritual or human exists—much less has any value—outside the State. In this respect Fascism is a totalizing concept, and the Fascist State—the unification and synthesis of every value—interprets, develops and potentiates the whole life of the people.

8. Conception of a Corporate State.

No individuals nor groups (political parties, associations, labour unions, classes) outside the State. For this reason Fascism is opposed to Socialism, which clings rigidly to class war in the historic evolution and ignores the unity of the State which moulds the classes into a single, moral and economic reality. In the same way Fascism is opposed to the unions of the labouring classes. But within the orbit of the State with ordinative functions, the real needs, which give rise to the Socialist movement and to the forming of labour unions, are emphatically recognized by Fascism and are given their full expression in the Corporative System, which conciliates every interest in the unity of the State.

9. Democracy.

Individuals form classes according to categories of interests. They are associated according to differentiated economical activities which have a common interest: but first and foremost they form the State. The State is not merely either the numbers or the sum of individuals forming the majority of a people. Fascism for this reason is opposed to the democracy which identifies peoples with the greatest number of individuals and reduces them to a majority level. But if people are conceived, as they should be, qualitatively and not quantitatively, then Fascism is democracy in its purest form. The qualitative conception is the most coherent and truest form and is therefore the most moral, because it sees a people realised in the consciousness and will of the few or even of one only; an ideal which moves to its realization in the consciousness and will of all. By "all" is meant all who derive their justification as a nation, ethnically speaking, from their nature and history, and who follow the same line of spiritual formation and development as one single will and consciousness— not as a race nor as a geographically determined region, but as a progeny that is rather the outcome of a history which perpetuates itself; a multitude unified by an idea embodied in the will to have power and to exist, conscious of itself and of its personality.

10. Conception of the State.

This higher personality is truly the nation, inasmuch as it is the State. The nation does not beget the State, according to the decrepit nationalistic concept which was used as a basis for the publicists of the national States in the Nineteenth Century. On the contrary, the nation is created by the State, which gives the people, conscious of their own moral unity, the will, and thereby an effective existence. The right of a nation to its independence is derived not from a literary and ideal consciousness of its own existence, much less from a de facto situation more or less inert and unconscious, but from an active consciousness, from an active political will disposed to demonstrate in its right; that is to say, a kind of State already in its pride (in fieri). The State, in fact, as a universal ethical will, is the creator of right.

11. Dynamic Reality.

The nation as a State is an ethical reality which exists and lives in measure as it develops. A standstill is its death. Therefore the State is not only the authority which governs and which gives the forms of law and the worth of the spiritual life to the individual wills, but it is also the power which gives effect to its will in foreign matters, causing it to be recognized and respected by demonstrating through facts the universality of all the manifestations necessary for its development. Hence it is organization as well as expansion, and it may be thereby considered, at least virtually, equal to the very nature of the human will, which in its evolution recognizes no barriers, and which realizes itself by proving its infinity.

12. The Role of the State.

The Fascist State, the highest and the most powerful form of personality is a force, but a spiritual one. It reassumes all the forms of the moral and intellectual life of man. It cannot, therefore, be limited to a simple function of order and of safeguarding, as was contended by Liberalism. It is not a simple mechanism which limits the sphere of the presumed individual liberties. It is an internal form and rule, a discipline of the entire person: it penetrates the will as well as the intelligence. Its principle, a central inspiration of the living human personality in the civil community, descends into the depths and settles in the heart of the man of action as well as the thinker, of the artist as well as of the scientist; the soul of our soul.

13. Discipline and Authority.

Fascism, in short, is not only a lawgiver and the founder of institutions, but an educator and a promoter of the spiritual life. It aims to rebuild not the forms of human life, but its content, the man, the character, the faith. And for this end it exacts discipline and an authority which descend into and dominates the interior of the spirit without opposition. Its emblem, therefore, is the *lictorian fasces*, symbol of unity, of force and of justice.

Political and Social Doctrine

1. Origins of the Doctrine.

When, in the now distant March of 1919, I summoned a meeting at Milan, through the columns of the *Popolo d'Italia*, of those who had supported and endured the war and who had followed me since the constitution of the *fasci* or Revolutionary Action in January 1915, there was no specific doctrinal plan in my mind. I had the experience of one only doctrine—that of Socialism from 1903-04 to the winter of 1914 about a decade—but I made it first in the ranks and later as a leader and it was never an experience in theory. My doctrine, even during that period, was a doctrine of action. A universally accepted doctrine of Socialism had not existed since 1915 when the revisionist movement started in Germany, under the leadership of Bernstein. Against this, in the swing of tendencies, a left revolutionary movement began to take shape, but in Italy it never went further than the "field of phrases," whereas in Russian Socialistic circles it became the prelude of Bolshevism. "Reformism," "revolutionarism," "centrism," this is a terminology of which even the echoes are now spent—but in the great river of Fascism are currents which flowed from Sorel, from Peguy, from Lagardelle and the *"Mouvement Socialiste,"* from Italian syndicalists which were legion between 1904 and 1914, and sounded a new note in Italian Socialist circles (weakened then by the betrayal of Giolitti) through Olivetti's Pagine *Libere*, Orano's *La Lupa* and Enrico Leone's *Divenire Sociale*.

After the War, in 1919, Socialism was already dead as a doctrine: it existed only as a grudge. In Italy especially, it had one only possibility of action: reprisals against those who had wanted the War and must now pay its penalty. The *Popolo d'Italia* carried as sub-title "daily of ex-service men and producers," and the word producers was already then the expression of a turn of mind. Fascism was not the nursling of a doctrine previously worked out at a desk; it was born of the need for action and it was action. It was not a party, in fact during the first two years, it was an anti-party and a movement.

The name I gave the organization fixed its character. Yet whoever should read the now crumpled sheets with the minutes of the meeting at which the Italian *"Fasci di Combattimento"* were constituted, would fail to discover a doctrine, but would find a series of ideas, of anticipations, of hints which, liberated from the inevitable strangleholds of contingencies, were destined after some years to develop into doctrinal conceptions. Through them Fascism became a political doctrine to itself, different, by comparison, to all others whether contemporary or of the past.

I said then, "If the bourgeoisie think we are ready to act as lightning-conductors, they are mistaken. We must go towards labour. We wish to train the working classes to directive functions. We wish to convince them that it is not easy to manage Industry or Trade: we shall fight the technique and the spirit of the rear-guard. When the succession of the regime is open, we must not lack the fighting spirit. We must rush and if the present regime be overcome, it is we who must fill its place. The claim to succession belongs to us, because it was we who forced the country into War and we who led her to victory. The present political representation cannot suffice: we must have a direct representation of all interest. Against this programme one might say it is a return to corporations. But that does not matter. Therefore I should like this assembly to accept the claims put in by national syndicalism from an economic standpoint...."

Is it not strange that the word corporations should have been uttered at the first meeting of Piazza San Sepolcro, when one considers that, in the course of the Revolution, it came to express one of the social and legislative creations at the very foundations of the regime?

2. Development.

The years which preceded the March on Rome were years in which the necessity of action did not permit complete doctrinal investigations or elaborations. The battle was raging in the towns and villages. There were discussions, but what was more important and sacred—there was death. Men knew how to die. The doctrine—all complete and formed, with divisions into chapters, paragraphs, and accompanying élucubrations—might be missing; but there was something more decided to replace it, there was faith.

Notwithstanding, whoever remembers with the aid of books and speeches, whoever could search through them and select, would find that the fundamental principles were laid down whilst the battle raged. It was really in those years that the Fascist idea armed itself, became refined and proceeded towards organization: the problems of the individual and of the State, the problems of authority and of liberty, the political and social problems, especially national; the fight against the liberal, democratic, socialistic and popular doctrines, was carried out together with the "punitive expeditions."

But as a "system" was lacking, our adversaries in bad faith, denied to Fascism any capacity to produce a doctrine, though that doctrine was growing tumultuously, at first under the aspect of violent and dogmatic negation, as happens to all newly-born ideas, and later under the positive aspect of construction which was successively realised, in the years 1926-27-28 through the laws and institutions of the regime. Fascism today stands clearly defined not only as a regime, but also as a doctrine. This word *doctrine* should be interpreted in the sense that Fascism, to-day, when passing criticism on itself and others, has its own point of view and its own point of reference, and therefore also its own orientation when facing those problems which beset the world in the spirit and in the matter.

3. Against Pacifism: War and Life as a Duty.

As far as the general future and development of humanity is concerned, and apart from any mere consideration of current politics, Fascism above all does not believe either in the possibility or utility of universal peace. It therefore rejects the pacifism which masks surrender and cowardice. War alone brings all human energies to their highest tension and sets a seal of nobility on the peoples who have the virtue to face it. All other tests are but substitutes which never make a man face himself in the alternative of life or death. A doctrine which has its starting-point at the prejudicial postulate of peace is therefore extraneous to Fascism.

In the same way all international creations (which, as history demonstrates, can be blown to the winds when sentimental, ideal and practical elements storm the heart of a people) are also extraneous to the spirit of Fascism—even if such international creations are accepted for whatever utility they may have in any determined political situation.

Fascism also transports this anti-pacifist spirit into the life of individuals. The proud squadrista motto *me ne frego* ("I don't give a damn") scrawled on the bandages of the wounded is an act of philosophy—not only stoic. It is a summary of a doctrine not only political: it is an education in strife and an acceptance of the risks which it carried: it is a new style of Italian life. It is thus that the Fascist loves and accepts life, ignores and disdains suicide; understands life as a duty, a lifting up, a conquest; something to be filled in and sustained on a high plane; a thing that has to be lived through for its own sake, but above all for the sake of others near and far, present and future.

4. The Demographic Policy and the "Neighbor."

The "demographic" policy of the regime is the result of these premises. The Fascist also loves his neighbor, but "neighbor" is not for him a vague and undefinable word: love for his neighbor does not prevent necessary educational severities. Fascism rejects professions of universal affection and, though living in the community of civilised peoples, it watches them and looks at them diffidently. It follows them in their state of mind and in the transformation of their interests, but it does not allow itself to be deceived by fallacious and mutable appearances.

5. Against Historical Materialism and Class-Struggle.

Through this conception of life Fascism becomes the emphatic negation of that doctrine which constituted the basis of the so-called scientific Socialism or Marxism: the doctrine of historical materialism, according to which the story of human civilisation is to be explained only by the conflict of interests between the various social groups and by the change of the means and instruments of production.

That the economic vicissitudes—discovery of prime or raw materials, new methods of labour, scientific inventions—have their particular importance, is denied by none, but that they suffice to explain human history, excluding other factors from it, is absurd: Fascism still believes in sanctity and in heroism, that is to say in acts in which no economic motive, immediate or remote, operates.

Fascism having denied historical materialism, by which men are only puppets in history, appearing and disappearing on the surface of the tides while in the depths the real directive forces act and labour, it also denies the immutable and irreparable class warfare, which is the natural filiation of such an economistic conception of history: and it denies above all that class warfare is the preponderating agent of social transformation. Being defeated on these two capital points of its doctrine, nothing remains of Socialism save the sentimental aspiration—as old as humanity—to achieve a community of social life in which the sufferings and hardships of the humblest classes are alleviated. But here Fascism repudiates the concept of an economic "happiness" which is to be—at a given moment in the evolution of economy—socialistically and almost automatically realised by assuring to all the maximum of well-being.

Fascism denies the possibilities of the materialistic concept of "happiness"—it leaves that to the economists of the first half of the Seventeenth Century; that is, it denies the equation "well-being-happiness," which reduces man to the state of the animals, mindful of only one thing—that of being fed and fattened; reduced, in fact, to a pure and simple vegetative existence.

6. Against Democratic Ideologies.

After disposing of Socialism, Fascism opens a breach on the whole complex of the democratic ideologies, and repudiates them in their theoretic premises as well as in their practical application or instrumentation. Fascism denies that numbers, by the mere fact of being numbers, can direct human society; it denies that these numbers can govern by means of periodical consultations; it affirms also the fertilizing, beneficent and unassailable inequality of men, who cannot be levelled through an extrinsic and mechanical process such as universal suffrage.

Regimes can be called democratic which, from time to time, give the people the illusion of being sovereign, whereas the real and effective sovereignty exists in other, and very often secret and irresponsible forces.

Democracy is a regime without a king, but very often with many kings, far more exclusive, tyrannical and ruinous than a single king, even if he be a tyrant. This explains why Fascism which, for contingent reasons, had assumed a republican tendency before 1922, renounced it previous to the March on Rome, with the conviction that the political constitution of a State is not nowadays a supreme question; and that, if the examples of past and present monarchies and past and present republics are studied, the result is that neither monarchies nor republics are to be judged under the assumption of eternity, but that they merely represent forms in which the extrinsic political evolution takes shape as well as the history, the tradition and the psychology of a given country.

Consequently, Fascism glides over the antithesis between monarchy and republic, on which democraticism wasted time, blaming the former for all social shortcomings and exalting the latter as a regime of perfection. We have now seen that there are republics which may be profoundly absolutist and reactionary, and monarchies which welcome the most venturesome social and political experiments.

7. Untruths of Democracy.

"Reason and science" says Renan (who had certain pre-fascist enlightenments) in one of his philosophical meditations, "are products of mankind, but to seek reason directly for the people and through the people is a chimera. It is not necessary for the existence of reason that everybody should know it. In any case if this initiation were to be brought about it could not be through low-class democracy, which seems to lead rather to the extinction of every difficult culture and of every great discipline. The principle that society exists only for the welfare and liberty of individuals composing it, does not seem to conform with the plans of nature: plans in which the species only is taken into consideration and the individual appears sacrificed. It is strongly to be feared that the last word of democracy thus understood (I hasten to add that it can also be differently understood) would be a social state in which a degenerated mass would have no preoccupation other than that of enjoying the ignoble pleasures of the vulgar person."

Thus Renan. In Democracy Fascism rejects the absurd conventional falsehood of political equality, the habit of collective responsibility and the myth of indefinite progress and happiness.

But if there be a different understanding of Democracy if, in other words, Democracy can also signify to not push the people back as far as the margins of the State, then Fascism may well have been defined by the present writer as "an organised, centralised, authoritarian Democracy."

8. Against Liberal Doctrines.

As regards the Liberal doctrines, the attitude of Fascism is one of absolute opposition both in the political and in the economical field. There is no need to exaggerate the importance of Liberalism in the last century—simply for the sake of present-day polemics—and to transform one of the numerous doctrines unfolded in that last century into a religion of humanity for all times, present and future. Liberalism did not flourish for more than a period of fifteen years. It was born in 1830 from the reaction to the Holy Alliance which attempted to set Europe back to the period which preceded '89 and had its years of splendor in 1848, when also Pius IX was a Liberal. Its decadence began immediately afterwards. If 1848 was a year of light and poesy, 1849 was a year of weakness and tragedy. The Roman Republic was killed by another Republic, the French Republic. In the same year Marx issued his famous manifesto of Communism. In 1851 Napoleon III made his anti-Liberal *coup d'état* and reigned over France until 1870. He was overthrown by a popular movement, following one of the greatest defeats registered in history. The victor was Bismarck, who always ignored the religion of liberty and its prophets. It is symptomatic that a people of high civilisation like the Germans completely ignored the religion of liberty throughout the whole Nineteenth Century—with but one parenthesis, represented by that which was called "the ridiculous parliament of Frankfurt" which lasted one season. Germany realised its national unity outside of Liberalism, against Liberalism—a doctrine which seemed alien to the German spirit essentially monarchical, since Liberalism is the historical and logical ante-chamber of anarchy.

The three wars of 1864, 1866 and 1870 conducted by "Liberals" like Moltke and Bismarck mark the three stages of German unity. As for Italian unity, Liberalism played a very inferior part in the make-up of Mazzini and Garibaldi, who were not liberals. Without the intervention of the anti-Liberal Napoleon we would not have had Lombardy, and without the help of the anti-Liberal Bismarck at Sadowa and Sedan it is very likely that we would not have got Venice in 1866, or that we would have entered Rome in 1870.

During the period of 1870-1915 the preachers of the new Credo themselves denounced the twilight of their religion; it was beaten in the breach by decadence in literature. It was beaten in the open by decadence in practice. Activism: that is to say, nationalism, futurism. Fascism.

The "Liberal Century" after having accumulated an infinity of Gordian knots, sought to cut them in the hecatomb of the World War. Never did any religion impose such a terrible sacrifice. Have the gods of Liberalism slaked their blood-thirst?

Liberalism is now on the point of closing the doors of its deserted temples because nations feel that its agnosticism in the economic field and its indifference in political and moral matters, causes, as it has already caused, the sure ruin of States. That is why all the political experiences of the contemporary world are anti-Liberal, and it is supremely silly to seek to classify them as things outside of history— as if history were a hunting ground reserved to Liberalism and its professors; as if Liberalism were the last and incomparable word of civilisation.

9. Fascism Does Not Turn Back.

The Fascist negation of Socialism, of Democracy, of Liberalism, should not lead one to believe that Fascism wishes to push the world back to where it was before 1879, the date accepted as the opening year of the demo-Liberal century. One cannot turn back. The Fascist doctrine has not chosen De Maistre for its prophet. Monarchical absolutism is a thing of the past, and so is the worship of church power. Feudal privileges and divisions into impenetrable castes with no connection between them, are also "have beens." The conception of Fascist authority has nothing in common with the Police. A party that totally rules a nation is a new chapter in history. References and comparisons are not possible. From the ruins of the socialist, liberal and democratic doctrines, Fascism picks those elements that still have a living value; keeps those that might be termed "facts acquired by history," and rejects the rest: namely the conception of a doctrine good for all times and all people.

Admitting that the Nineteenth Century was the Century of Socialism, Liberalism and Democracy, it is not said that the Twentieth century must also be the century of Socialism, of Liberalism, of Democracy. Political doctrines pass on, but peoples remain. One may now think that this will be the century of authority, the century of the "right wing" the century of Fascism. If the Nineteenth Century was the century of the individual (liberalism signifies individualism) one may think that this will be the century of "collectivism," the century of the State. It is perfectly logical that a new doctrine should utilise the vital elements of other doctrines. No doctrine was ever born entirely new and shining, never seen before. No doctrine can boast of absolute "originality." Each doctrine is bound historically to doctrines which went before, to doctrines yet to come. Thus the scientific Socialism of Marx is bound to the Utopian Socialism of Fourier, of Owen, of Saint-Simon; thus the Liberalism of 1800 is linked with the movement of 1700. Thus Democratic doctrines are bound to the Encyclopaedists. Each doctrine tends to direct human activity towards a definite object; but the activity of man reacts upon the doctrine, transforms it and adapts it to new requirements, or overcomes it. Doctrine therefore should be an act of life and not an academy of words. In this lie the pragmatic veins of Fascism, its will to power, its will to be, its position with regard to "violence" and its value.

10. The Value and Mission of the State.

The capital point of the Fascist doctrine is the conception of the State, its essence, the work to be accomplished, its final aims. In the conception of Fascism, the State is an absolute before which individuals and groups are relative. Individuals and groups are "conceivable" inasmuch as they are in the State. The Liberal State does not direct the movement and the material and spiritual evolution of collectivity, but limits itself to recording the results; the Fascist State has its conscious conviction, a will of its own, and for this reason it is called an "ethical" State.

In 1929 at the first quinquennial assembly of the Regime, I said: "In Fascism the State is not a night-watchman, only occupied with the personal safety of the citizens, nor is it an organization with purely material aims, such as that of assuring a certain well-being and a comparatively easy social cohabitation. A board of directors would be quite sufficient to deal with this. It is not a purely political creation, either, detached from the complex material realities of the life of individuals and of peoples. The State as conceived and enacted by Fascism, is a spiritual and moral fact since it gives concrete form to the political, juridical and economical organization of the country. Furthermore this organization as it rises and develops, is a manifestation of the spirit.

The State is a safeguard of interior and exterior safety but it is also the keeper and the transmitter of the spirit of the people, as it was elaborated throughout the ages, in its language, customs and beliefs.

The State is not only the present, but it is also the past and above all the future. The State, inasmuch as it transcends the short limits of individual lives, represents the immanent conscience of the nation. The forms in which the State expresses itself are subject to changes, but the necessity for the State remains. It is the State which educates the citizens in civic virtues, gives them a consciousness of their mission, presses them towards unity; the State harmonizes their interests through justice, transmits to prosperity the attainments of thoughts, in science, in art, in laws, in the solidarity of mankind. The State leads men from primitive tribal life to that highest expression of human power which is Empire; links up through the centuries the names of those who died to preserve its integrity or to obey its laws; holds up the memory of the leaders who increased its territory, and of the geniuses who cast the light of glory upon it, as an example for future generations to follow. When the conception of the State declines and disintegrating or centrifugal tendencies prevail, whether of individuals or groups, then the national society is about to set."

11. The Unity of the State and the Contradictions of Capitalism.

From 1929 onwards to the present day, the universal, political and economical evolution has still further strengthened the doctrinal positions. The giant who rules is the State. The one who can resolve the dramatic contradictions of capital is the State. What is called the crisis cannot be resolved except by the State and in the State. Where are the ghosts of Jules Simon who, at the dawn of Liberalism, proclaimed that "the State must set to work to make itself useless and prepare its resignation?" Of MacCulloch who, in the second half of the past century, proclaimed that the State must abstain from ruling? What would the Englishman Bentham say today to the continual and inevitably-invoked intervention of the State in the sphere of economics, while, according to his theories, industry should ask no more of the State than to be left in peace? Or the German Humboldt according to whom an "idle" State was the best kind of State? It is true that the second wave of Liberal economists were less extreme than the first, and Adam Smith himself opened the door—if only very cautiously—to let State intervention into the economic field.

If Liberalism signifies the individual—then Fascism signifies the State. But the Fascist State is unique of its kind and is an original creation. It is not reactionary but revolutionary, inasmuch as it anticipates the solution of certain universal problems such as those which are treated elsewhere:

1. in the political sphere, by the subdivisions of parties, in the preponderance of parliamentarism and in the irresponsibilities of assemblies;

2. in the economic sphere, by the functions of trade unions which are becoming constantly more numerous and powerful, whether in the labour or industrial fields, in their conflicts and combinations, and

3. in the moral sphere by the necessity of order, discipline, obedience to those who are the moral dictators of the country. Fascism wants the State to be strong, organic and at the same time supported on a wide popular basis. As part of its task the Fascist State has penetrated the economic field: through the corporative, social and educational institutions which it has created. The presence of the State is felt in the remotest ramifications of the country. And in the State also, all the political, economic and spiritual forces of the nation circulate, mustered in their respective organizations.

A State which stands on the support of millions of individuals who recognise it, who believe in it, who are ready to serve it, is not the tyrannical State of the mediaeval lord. It has nothing in common with the absolutist States before or after '89. The individual in the Fascist State is not annulled but rather multiplied, just as in a regiment a soldier is not diminished, but multiplied by the number of his comrades.

The Fascist State organises the nation, but leaves a sufficient margin afterward to the individual; it has limited the useless or harmful liberties and has preserved the essential ones. The one to judge in this respect is not the individual but the State.

12. The Fascist State and Religion.

The Fascist State is not indifferent to the presence or the fact of religion in general nor to the presence of that particular established religion, which is Italian Catholicism. The State has no theology, but it has morality. In the Fascist State religion is considered as one of the most profound manifestations of the spirit; it is therefore not only respected, but defended and protected. The Fascist State does not create its own "God," as Robespierre wanted to do at a certain moment in the frenzies of the Convention; nor does it vainly endeavour to cancel the idea of God from the mind as Bolshevism tries to do. Fascism respects the God of the ascetics, of the saints and of the heroes. It also respects God as he is conceived and prayed to in the ingenuous and primitive heart of the people.

13. Empire and Discipline.

The Fascist State is a will expressing power and empire. The Roman tradition here becomes an idea of force. In the Fascist doctrine, empire is not only a territorial or a military, or a commercial expression: it is a moral and a spiritual one. An empire can be thought of, for instance, as a nation which directly or indirectly guides other nations—without the need of conquering a single mile of territory. For Fascism, the tendency to empire, that is to say the expansion of nations, is a manifestation of vitality, its contrary (the stay-at-home attitude) is a sign of decadence. Peoples who rise, or who suddenly flourish again, are imperialistic; peoples who die are peoples who abdicate. Fascism is a doctrine which most adequately represents the tendencies, the state of mind of a people like the Italian people, which is rising again after many centuries of abandonment and of foreign servitude.

But empire requires discipline, the coordination of forces, duty and sacrifice. This explains many phases of the practical action of the regime. It explains the aims of many of the forces of the State and the necessary severity against those who would oppose themselves to this spontaneous and irresistible movement of the Italy of the Twentieth century by trying to appeal to the discredited ideologies of the Nineteenth century, which have been repudiated wherever great experiments of political and social transformation have been daringly undertaken.

Never more than at the present moment have the nations felt such a thirst for an authority, for a direction, for order. If every century has its own peculiar doctrine, there are a thousand indications that Fascism is that of the present century. That it is a doctrine of life is shown by the fact that it has created a faith; that the faith has taken possession of the mind is demonstrated by the fact that Fascism has had its Fallen and its martyrs.

Fascism has now attained in the world an universality over all doctrines. Being realised, it represents an epoch in the history of the human mind.

The Political Doctrine of Fascism

Alfredo Rocco

Premier Mussolini's Endorsement
of Signor Rocco's Speech

The following message was sent by Benito Mussolini, the Premier of Italy, to Signor Rocco after he had delivered his speech at Perugia.

Dear Rocco,

I have just read your magnificent address which I endorse throughout. You have presented in a masterful way the doctrine of Fascism. For Fascism has a doctrine, or, if you will, a particular philosophy with regard to all the questions which beset the human mind today. All Italian Fascists should read your discourse and derive from it both the clear formulation of the basic principles of our program as well as the reasons why Fascism must be systematically, firmly, and rationally inflexible in its uncompromising attitude towards other parties. Thus and only thus can the word become flesh and the ideas be turned into deeds.

Cordial greetings,

Mussolini.

The Political Doctrine of Fascism

Fascism as Action, Feeling, and Thought

Much has been said, and is now being said for or against this complex political and social phenomenon which in the brief period of six years has taken complete hold of Italian life and, spreading beyond the borders of the Kingdom, has made itself felt in varying degrees of intensity throughout the world. But people have been much more eager to extol or to deplore than to understand—which is natural enough in a period of tumultuous fervor and of political passion. The time has not yet arrived for a dispassionate judgment. For even I, who noticed the very first manifestations of this great development, saw its significance from the start and participated directly in its first doings, carefully watching all its early uncertain and changing developments, even I do not feel competent to pass definite judgment.

Fascism is so large a part of myself that it would be both arbitrary and absurd for me to try to dissociate my personality from it, to submit it to impartial scrutiny in order to evaluate it coldly and accurately. What can be done, however, and it seldom is attempted, is to make inquiry into the phenomenon which shall not merely consider its fragmentary and adventitious aspects, but strive to get at its inner essence. The undertaking may not be easy, but it is necessary, and no occasion for attempting it is more suitable than the present one afforded me by my friends of Perugia. Suitable it is in time because, at the inauguration of a course of lectures and lessons principally intended to illustrate that old and glorious trend of the life and history of Italy which takes its name from the humble saint of Assisi, it seemed natural to connect it with the greatest achievement of modern Italy, different in so many ways from the Franciscan movement, but united with it by the mighty common current of Italian History. It is suitable as well in place because at Perugia, which witnessed the growth of our religious ideas, of our political doctrines and of our legal science in the course of the most glorious centuries of our cultural history, the mind is properly disposed and almost oriented towards an investigation of this nature.

First of all let us ask ourselves if there is a political doctrine of Fascism; if there is any ideal content in the Fascist state. For in order to link Fascism, both as concept and system, with the history of Italian thought and find therein a place for it, we must first show that it is thought; that it is a doctrine. Many persons are not quite convinced that it is either the one or the other; and I am not referring solely to those men, cultured or uncultured, as the case may be and very numerous everywhere, who can discern in this political innovation nothing except its local and personal aspects, and who know Fascism only as the particular manner of behavior of this or that well-known Fascist, of this or that group of a certain town; who therefore like or dislike the movement on the basis of their likes and dislikes for the individuals who represent it. Nor do I refer to those intelligent, and cultivated persons, very intelligent indeed and very cultivated, who because of their direct or indirect allegiance to the parties that have been dispossessed by the advent of Fascism, have a natural cause of resentment against it and are therefore unable to see, in the blindness of hatred, anything good in it. I am referring rather to those—and there are many in our ranks too—who know Fascism as action and feeling but not yet as thought, who therefore have an intuition but no comprehension of it.

It is true that Fascism is, above all, action and sentiment and that such it must continue to be. Were it otherwise, it could not keep up that immense driving force, that renovating power which it now possesses and would merely be the solitary meditation of a chosen few. Only because it is feeling and sentiment, only because it is the unconscious reawakening of our profound racial instinct, has it the force to stir the soul of the people, and to set free an irresistible current of national will. Only because it is action, and as such actualizes itself in a vast organization and in a huge movement, has it the conditions for determining the historical course of contemporary Italy.

But Fascism is thought as well and it has a theory, which is an essential part of this historical phenomenon, and which is responsible in a great measure for the successes that have been achieved. To the existence of this ideal content of Fascism, to the truth of this Fascist logic we ascribe the fact that though we commit many errors of detail, we very seldom go astray on fundamentals, whereas all the parties of the opposition, deprived as they are of an informing, animating principle, of a unique directing concept, do very often wage their war faultlessly in minor tactics, better trained as they are in parliamentary and journalistic manoeuvres, but they constantly break down on the important issues. Fascism, moreover, considered as action, is a typically Italian phenomenon and acquires a universal validity because of the existence of this coherent and organic doctrine. The originality of Fascism is due in great part to the autonomy of its theoretical principles. For even when, in its external behavior and in its conclusions, it seems identical with other political creeds, in reality it possesses an inner originality due to the new spirit which animates it and to an entirely different theoretical approach.

The Political Doctrine of Fascism

Common Origins and Common Background of Modern Political Doctrines: From Liberalism to Socialism

Modern political thought remained, until recently, both in Italy and outside of Italy under the absolute control of those doctrines which, proceeding from the Protestant Reformation and developed by the adepts of natural law in the XVII and XVIII centuries, were firmly grounded in the institutions and customs of the English, of the American, and of the French Revolutions. Under different and sometimes clashing forms these doctrines have left a determining imprint upon all theories and actions both social and political, of the XIX and XX centuries down to the rise of Fascism. The common basis of all these doctrines, which stretch from Longuet, from Buchanan, and from Althusen down to Karl Marx, to Wilson and to Lenin is a social and state concept which I shall call mechanical or atomistic.

Society according to this concept is merely a sum total of individuals, a plurality which breaks up into its single components. Therefore the ends of a society, so considered, are nothing more than the ends of the individuals which compose it and for whose sake it exists. An atomistic view of this kind is also necessarily anti-historical, inasmuch as it considers society in its spatial attributes and not in its temporal ones; and because it reduces social life to the existence of a single generation. Society becomes thus a sum of determined individuals, viz., the generation living at a given moment. This doctrine which I call atomistic and which appears to be anti-historical, reveals from under a concealing cloak a strongly materialistic nature. For in its endeavors to isolate the present from the past and the future, it rejects the spiritual inheritance of ideas and sentiments which each generation receives from those preceding and hands down to the following generation thus destroying the unity and the spiritual life itself of human society.

This common basis shows the close logical connection existing between all political doctrines; the substantial solidarity, which unites all the political movements, from Liberalism to Socialism, that until recently have dominated Europe. For these political schools differ from one another in their methods, but all agree as to the ends to be achieved. All of them consider the welfare and happiness of individuals to be the goal of society, itself considered as composed of individuals of the present generation. All of them see in society and in its juridical organization, the state, the mere instrument and means whereby individuals can attain their ends. They differ only in that the

49

methods pursued for the attainment of these ends vary considerably one from the other.

Thus the Liberals insist that the best manner to secure the welfare of the citizens as individuals is to interfere as little as possible with the free development of their activities and that therefore the essential task of the state is merely to coordinate these several liberties in such a way as to guarantee their coexistence. Kant, who was without doubt the most powerful and thorough philosopher of liberalism, said, "man, who is the end, cannot be assumed to have the value of an instrument." And again, "justice, of which the state is the specific organ, is the condition whereby the freedom of each is conditioned upon the freedom of others, according to the general law of liberty."

Having thus defined the task of the state, Liberalism confines itself to the demand of certain guarantees which are to keep the state from overstepping its functions as general coordinator of liberties and from sacrificing the freedom of individuals more than is absolutely necessary for the accomplishment of its purpose. All the efforts are therefore directed to see to it that the ruler, mandatory of all and entrusted with the realization, through and by liberty, of the harmonious happiness of everybody, should never be clothed with undue power. Hence the creation of a system of checks and limitations designed to keep the rulers within bounds; and among these, first and foremost, the principle of the division of powers, contrived as a means for weakening the state in its relation to the individual, by making it impossible for the state ever to appear, in its dealings with citizens, in the full plenitude of sovereign powers; also the principle of the participation of citizens in the lawmaking power, as a means for securing, in behalf of the individual, a direct check on this, the strongest branch, and an indirect check on the entire government of the state. This system of checks and limitations, which goes by the name of constitutional government resulted in a moderate and measured liberalism. The checking power was exercised only by those citizens who were deemed worthy and capable, with the result that a small élite was made to represent legally the entire body politic for whose benefit this régime was instituted.

It was evident, however, that this moderate system, being fundamentally illogical and in contradiction with the very principles from which it proceeded, would soon become the object of serious criticism. For if the object of society and of the state is the welfare of individuals, severally considered, how is it possible to admit that this welfare can be secured by the individuals themselves only through the possibilities of such a liberal régime? The inequalities brought about both by nature and by social organizations are so numerous and so serious, that, for the greater part, individuals abandoned to themselves not only would fail to attain happiness, but would also contribute to the perpetuation of their condition of misery and dejection. The state therefore cannot limit itself to the merely negative function of the defense of liberty. It must become active, in behalf of everybody, for the welfare of the people. It must intervene, when necessary, in order to improve the material, intellectual, and moral conditions of the masses; it must find work for the unemployed, instruct and educate the people, and care for health and hygiene. For if the purpose of society and of the state is the welfare of individuals, and if it is just that these individuals themselves control the attainment of their ends, it becomes difficult to understand why Liberalism should not go the whole distance, why it should see fit to distinguish certain individuals from the rest of the mass, and why the functions of the people should be restricted to the exercise of a mere check. Therefore the state, if it exists for all, must be governed by all, and not by a small minority: if the state is for the people, sovereignty must reside in the people: if all individuals have the right to govern the state, liberty is no longer sufficient; equality must be added: and if sovereignty is vested in the people, the people must wield all sovereignty and not merely a part of it. The power to check and curb the government is not sufficient. The people must be the government. Thus, logically developed, Liberalism leads to Democracy, for Democracy contains the promises of Liberalism but oversteps its limitations in that it makes the action of the state positive, proclaims the equality of all citizens through the dogma of popular sovereignty. Democracy therefore necessarily implies a republican form of government even though at times, for reasons of expediency, it temporarily adjusts itself to a monarchical régime.

Once started on this downward grade of logical deductions it was inevitable that this atomistic theory of state and society should pass on to a more advanced position. Great industrial developments and the existence of a huge mass of working men, as yet badly treated and in a condition of semi-servitude, possibly endurable in a régime of domestic industry, became intolerable after the industrial revolution. Hence a state of affairs which towards the middle of the last century appeared to be both cruel and threatening. It was therefore natural that the following question be raised: "If the state is created for the welfare of its citizens, severally considered, how can it tolerate an economic system which divides the population into a small minority of exploiters, the capitalists, on one side, and an immense multitude of exploited, the working people, on the other?" No! The state must again intervene and give rise to a different and less iniquitous economic organization, by abolishing private property, by assuming direct control of all production, and by organizing it in such a way that the products of labor be distributed solely among those who create them, viz., the working classes. Hence we find Socialism, with its new economic organization of society, abolishing private ownership of capital and of the instruments and means of production, socializing the product, suppressing the extra profit of capital, and turning over to the working class the entire output of the productive processes. It is evident that Socialism contains and surpasses Democracy in the same way that Democracy comprises and surpasses Liberalism, being a more advanced development of the same fundamental concept. Socialism in its turn generates the still more extreme doctrine of Bolshevism which demands the violent suppression of the holders of capital, the dictatorship of the proletariat, as means for a fairer economic organization of society and for the rescue of the laboring classes from capitalistic exploitation.

Thus Liberalism, Democracy, and Socialism, appear to be, as they are in reality, not only the offspring of one and the same theory of government, but also logical derivations one of the other. Logically developed Liberalism leads to Democracy; the logical development of Democracy issues into Socialism. It is true that for many years, and with some justification, Socialism was looked upon as antithetical to Liberalism. But the antithesis is purely relative and breaks down as we approach the common origin and foundation of the two doctrines, for we find that the opposition is one of method, not of purpose. The end is the same for both, viz., the welfare of the individual members of society. The difference lies in the fact that Liberalism would be guided to its goal by liberty, whereas Socialism strives to attain it by the collective organization of production. There is therefore no antithesis nor even a divergence as to the nature and scope of the state and the relation of individuals to society. There is only a difference of evaluation of the means for bringing about these ends and establishing these relations, which difference depends entirely on the different economic conditions which prevailed at the time when the various doctrines were formulated. Liberalism arose and began to thrive in the period of small industry; Socialism grew with the rise of industrialism and of world-wide capitalism. The dissension therefore between these two points of view, or the antithesis, if we wish so to call it, is limited to the economic field. Socialism is at odds with Liberalism only on the question of the organization of production and of the division of wealth. In religious, intellectual, and moral matters it is liberal, as it is liberal and democratic in its politics. Even the anti-liberalism and anti-democracy of Bolshevism are in themselves purely contingent. For Bolshevism is opposed to Liberalism only in so far as the former is revolutionary, not in its socialistic aspect. For if the opposition of the Bolsheviki to liberal and democratic doctrines were to continue, as now seems more and more probable, the result might be a complete break between Bolshevism and Socialism notwithstanding the fact that the ultimate aims of both are identical.

Fascism as an Integral Doctrine of Sociality Antithetical to the Atomism of Liberal, Democratic, and Socialistic Theories

The true antithesis, not to this or that manifestation of the liberal-democratic-socialistic conception of the state but to the concept itself, is to be found in the doctrine of Fascism. For while the disagreement between Liberalism and Democracy, and between Liberalism and Socialism lies in a difference of method, as we have said, the rift between Socialism, Democracy, and Liberalism on one side and Fascism on the other is caused by a difference in concept. As a matter of fact, Fascism never raises the question of methods, using in its political praxis now liberal ways, now democratic means and at times even socialistic devices. This indifference to method often exposes Fascism to the charge of incoherence on the part of superficial observers, who do not see that what counts with us is the end and that therefore even when we employ the same means we act with a radically different spiritual attitude and strive for entirely different results. The Fascist concept then of the nation, of the scope of the state, and of the relations obtaining between society and its individual components, rejects entirely the doctrine which I said proceeded from the theories of natural law developed in the course of the 16th, 17th, and 18th centuries and which form the basis of the liberal, democratic, and socialistic ideology.

I shall not try here to expound this doctrine but shall limit myself to a brief résumé of its fundamental concepts.

Man—the political animal—according to the definition of Aristotle, lives and must live in society. A human being outside the pale of society is an inconceivable thing—a non-man. Humankind in its entirety lives in social groups that are still, today, very numerous and diverse, varying in importance and organization from the tribes of Central Africa to the great Western Empires. These various societies are fractions of the human species each one of them endowed with a unified organization. And as there is no unique organization of the human species, there is not "one" but there are "several" human societies. Humanity therefore exists solely as a biological concept not as a social one.

Each society on the other hand exists in the unity of both its biological and its social contents. Socially considered it is a fraction of the human species endowed with unity of organization for the attainment of the peculiar ends of the species.

This definition brings out all the elements of the social phenomenon and not merely those relating to the preservation and perpetuation of the species. For man is not solely matter; and the ends of the human species, far from being the materialistic ones we have in common with other animals, are, rather, and predominantly, the spiritual finalities which are peculiar to man and which every form of society strives to attain as well as its stage of social development allows. Thus the organization of every social group is more or less pervaded by the spiritual influxes of: unity of language, of culture, of religion, of tradition, of customs, and in general of feeling and of volition, which are as essential as the material elements: unity of economic interests, of living conditions, and of territory. The definition given above demonstrates another truth, which has been ignored by the political doctrines that for the last four centuries have been the foundations of political systems, viz., that the social concept has a biological aspect, because social groups are fractions of the human species, each one possessing a peculiar organization, a particular rank in the development of civilization with certain needs and appropriate ends, in short, a life which is really its own. If social groups are then fractions of the human species, they must possess the same fundamental traits of the human species, which means that they must be considered as a succession of generations and not as a collection of individuals.

It is evident therefore that as the human species is not the total of the living human beings of the world, so the various social groups which compose it are not the sum of the several individuals which at a given moment belong to it, but rather the infinite series of the past, present, and future generations constituting it. And as the ends of the human species are not those of the several individuals living at a certain moment, being occasionally in direct opposition to them, so the ends of the various social groups are not necessarily those of the individuals that belong to the groups but may even possibly be in conflict with such ends, as one sees clearly whenever the preservation and the development of the species demand the sacrifice of the individual, to wit, in times of war.

Fascism replaces therefore the old atomistic and mechanical state theory which was at the basis of the liberal and democratic doctrines with an organic and historic concept. When I say organic I do not wish to convey the impression that I consider society as an organism after the manner of the so-called "organic theories of the state"; but rather to indicate that the social groups as fractions of the species receive thereby a life and scope which transcend the scope and life of the individuals identifying themselves with the history and finalities of the uninterrupted series of generations. It is irrelevant in this connection to determine whether social groups, considered as fractions of the species, constitute organisms. The important thing is to ascertain that this organic concept of the state gives to society a continuous life over and beyond the existence of the several individuals.

The relations therefore between state and citizens are completely reversed by the Fascist doctrine. Instead of the liberal-democratic formula, "society for the individual," we have, "individuals for society" with this difference however: that while the liberal doctrines eliminated society, Fascism does not submerge the individual in the social group. It subordinates him, but does not eliminate him; the individual as a part of his generation ever remaining an element of society however transient and insignificant he may be. Moreover the development of individuals in each generation, when coordinated and harmonized, conditions the development and prosperity of the entire social unit.

At this juncture the antithesis between the two theories must appear complete and absolute. Liberalism, Democracy, and Socialism look upon social groups as aggregates of living individuals; for Fascism they are the recapitulating unity of the indefinite series of generations. For Liberalism, society has no purposes other than those of the members living at a given moment. For Fascism, society has historical and immanent ends of preservation, expansion, improvement, quite distinct from those of the individuals which at a given moment compose it; so distinct in fact that they may even be in opposition. Hence the necessity, for which the older doctrines make little allowance, of sacrifice, even up to the total immolation of individuals, in behalf of society; hence the true explanation of war, eternal law of mankind, interpreted by the liberal-democratic doctrines as a degenerate absurdity or as a maddened monstrosity.

For Liberalism, society has no life distinct from the life of the individuals, or as the phrase goes: *solvitur in singularitates*. For Fascism, the life of society overlaps the existence of individuals and projects itself into the succeeding generations through centuries and millennia. Individuals come into being, grow, and die, followed by others, unceasingly; social unity remains always identical to itself. For Liberalism, the individual is the end and society the means; nor is it conceivable that the individual, considered in the dignity of an ultimate finality, be lowered to mere instrumentality. For Fascism, society is the end, individuals the means, and its whole life consists in using individuals as instruments for its social ends. The state therefore guards and protects the welfare and development of individuals not for their exclusive interest, but because of the identity of the needs of individuals with those of society as a whole. We can thus accept and explain institutions and practices, which like the death penalty, are condemned by Liberalism in the name of the preeminence of individualism.

The fundamental problem of society in the old doctrines is the question of the rights of individuals. It may be the right to freedom as the Liberals would have it; or the right to the government of the commonwealth as the Democrats claim it, or the right to economic justice as the Socialists contend; but in every case it is the right of individuals, or groups of individuals (classes). Fascism on the other hand faces squarely the problem of the right of the state and of the duty of individuals. Individual rights are only recognized in so far as they are implied in the rights of the state. In this preeminence of duty we find the highest ethical value of Fascism.

The Problems of Liberty, of Government, and of Social Justice in the Political Doctrine of Fascism

This, however, does not mean that the problems raised by the other schools are ignored by Fascism. It means simply that it faces them and solves them differently, as, for example, the problem of liberty.

There is a Liberal theory of freedom, and there is a Fascist concept of liberty. For we, too, maintain the necessity of safeguarding the conditions that make for the free development of the individual; we, too, believe that the oppression of individual personality can find no place in the modern state. We do not, however, accept a bill of rights which tends to make the individual superior to the state and to empower him to act in opposition to society. Our concept of liberty is that the individual must be allowed to develop his personality in behalf of the state, for these ephemeral and infinitesimal elements of the complex and permanent life of society determine by their normal growth the development of the state. But this individual growth must be normal. A huge and disproportionate development of the individual of classes, would prove as fatal to society as abnormal growths are to living organisms. Freedom therefore is due to the citizen and to classes on condition that they exercise it in the interest of society as a whole and within the limits set by social exigencies, liberty being, like any other individual right, a concession of the state. What I say concerning civil liberties applies to economic freedom as well. Fascism does not look upon the doctrine of economic liberty as an absolute dogma. It does not refer economic problems to individual needs, to individual interest, to individual solutions. On the contrary it considers the economic development, and especially the production of wealth, as an eminently social concern, wealth being for society an essential element of power and prosperity. But Fascism maintains that in the ordinary run of events economic liberty serves the social purposes best; that it is profitable to entrust to individual initiative the task of economic development both as to production and as to distribution; that in the economic world individual ambition is the most effective means for obtaining the best social results with the least effort. Therefore, on the question also of economic liberty the Fascists differ fundamentally from the Liberals; the latter see in liberty a principle, the Fascists accept it as a method. By the Liberals, freedom is recognized in the interest of the citizens; the Fascists grant it in the interest of society. In other terms, Fascists make of the individual an economic instrument for the advancement of society, an instrument which they use so long as it functions and which they subordinate when no longer serviceable. In this guise Fascism solves the eternal problem of economic freedom and of state interference, considering both as mere methods which may or may not be employed in accordance with the social needs of the moment.

What I have said concerning political and economic Liberalism applies also to Democracy. The latter envisages fundamentally the problem of sovereignty; Fascism does also, but in an entirely different manner. Democracy vests sovereignty in the people, that is to say, in the mass of human beings. Fascism discovers sovereignty to be inherent in society when it is juridically organized as a state. Democracy therefore turns over the government of the state to the multitude of living men that they may use it to further their own interests; Fascism insists that the government be entrusted to men capable of rising above their own private interests and of realizing the aspirations of the social collectivity, considered in its unity and in its relation to the past and future. Fascism therefore not only rejects the dogma of popular sovereignty and substitutes for it that of state sovereignty, but it also proclaims that the great mass of citizens is not a suitable advocate of social interests for the reason that the capacity to ignore individual private interests in favor of the higher demands of society and of history is a very rare gift and the privilege of the chosen few. Natural intelligence and cultural preparation are of great service in such tasks. Still more valuable perhaps is the intuitiveness of rare great minds, their traditionalism and their inherited qualities. This must not however be construed to mean that the masses are not to be allowed to exercise any influence on the life of the state. On the contrary, among peoples with a great history and with noble traditions, even the lowest elements of society possess an instinctive discernment of what is necessary for the welfare of the race, which in moments of great historical crises reveals itself to be almost infallible. It is therefore as wise to afford to this instinct the means of declaring itself as it is judicious to entrust the normal control of the commonwealth to a selected élite.

As for Socialism, the Fascist doctrine frankly recognizes that the problem raised by it as to the relations between capital and labor is a very serious one, perhaps the central one of modern life. What Fascism does not countenance is the collectivistic solution proposed by the Socialists. The chief defect of the socialistic method has been clearly demonstrated by the experience of the last few years. It does not take into account human nature, it is therefore outside of reality, in that it will not recognize that the most powerful spring of human activities lies in individual self-interest and that therefore the elimination from the economic field of this interest results in complete paralysis. The suppression of private ownership of capital carries with it the suppression of capital itself, for capital is formed by savings and no one will want to save, but will rather consume all he makes if he knows he cannot keep and hand down to his heirs the results of his labors. The dispersion of capital means the end of production since capital, no matter who owns it, is always an indispensable tool of production.

Collective organization of production is followed therefore by the paralysis of production since, by eliminating from the productive mechanism the incentive of individual interest, the product becomes rarer and more costly. Socialism then, as experience has shown, leads to increase in consumption, to the dispersion of capital and therefore to poverty. Of what avail is it, then, to build a social machine which will more justly distribute wealth if this very wealth is destroyed by the construction of this machine? Socialism committed an irreparable error when it made of private property a matter of justice while in truth it is a problem of social utility. The recognition of individual property rights, then, is a part of the Fascist doctrine not because of its individual bearing but because of its social utility.

We must reject, therefore, the socialistic solution but we cannot allow the problem raised by the Socialists to remain unsolved, not only because justice demands a solution but also because the persistence of this problem in liberal and democratic régimes has been a menace to public order and to the authority of the state. Unlimited and unrestrained class self-defense, evinced by strikes and lockouts, by boycotts and sabotage, leads inevitably to anarchy. The Fascist doctrine, enacting justice among the classes in compliance with a fundamental necessity of modern life, does away with class self-defense, which, like individual self-defense in the days of barbarism, is a source of disorder and of civil war.

Having reduced the problem of these terms, only one solution is possible, the realization of justice among the classes by and through the state. Centuries ago the state, as the specific organ of justice, abolished personal self-defense in individual controversies and substituted for it state justice. The time has now come when class self-defense also must be replaced by state justice. To facilitate the change Fascism has created its own syndicalism. The suppression of class self-defense does not mean the suppression of class defense which is an inalienable necessity of modern economic life. Class organization is a fact which cannot be ignored but it must be controlled, disciplined, and subordinated by the state. The syndicate, instead of being, as formerly, an organ of extra-legal defense, must be turned into an organ of legal defense which will become judicial defense as soon as labor conflicts become a matter of judicial settlement. Fascism therefore has transformed the syndicate, that old revolutionary instrument of syndicalistic socialists, into an instrument of legal defense of the classes both within and without the law courts. This solution may encounter obstacles in its development; the obstacles of malevolence, of suspicion of the untried, of erroneous calculation, etc., but it is destined to triumph even though it must advance through progressive stages.

Historical Value of the Doctrine of Fascism

I might carry this analysis farther but what I have already said is sufficient to show that the rise of a Fascist ideology already gives evidence of an upheaval in the intellectual field as powerful as the change that was brought about in the 17th and 18th centuries by the rise and diffusion of those doctrines of ius naturale which go under the name of "Philosophy of the French Revolution." The philosophy of the French Revolution formulated certain principles, the authority of which, unquestioned for a century and a half, seemed so final that they were given the attribute of immortality. The influence of these principles was so great that they determined the formation of a new culture, of a new civilization. Likewise the fervor of the ideas that go to make up the Fascist doctrine, now in its inception but destined to spread rapidly, will determine the course of a new culture and of a new conception of civil life. The deliverance of the individual from the state carried out in the 18th century will be followed in the 20th century by the rescue of the state from the individual. The period of authority, of social obligations, of "hierarchical" subordination will succeed the period of individualism, of state feebleness, of insubordination.

This innovating trend is not and cannot be a return to the Middle Ages. It is a common but an erroneous belief that the movement, started by the Reformation and heightened by the French Revolution, was directed against mediaeval ideas and institutions. Rather than as a negation, this movement should be looked upon as the development and fulfillment of the doctrines and practices of the Middle Ages. Socially and politically considered the Middle Ages wrought disintegration and anarchy; they were characterized by the gradual weakening and ultimate extinction of the state, embodied in the Roman Empire, driven first to the East, then back to France, thence to Germany, a shadow of its former self; they were marked by the steady advance of the forces of usurpation, destructive of the state and reciprocally obnoxious; they bore the imprints of a triumphant particularism. Therefore the individualistic and anti-social movement of the 17th and 18th centuries was not directed against the Middle Ages, but rather against the restoration of the state by great national monarchies. If this movement destroyed mediaeval institutions that had survived the Middle Ages and had been grafted upon the new states, it was in consequence of the struggle primarily waged against the state. The spirit of the movement was decidedly mediaeval. The novelty consisted in the social surroundings in which it operated and in its relation to new economic developments. The individualism of the feudal lords, the particularism of the cities and of the corporations had been replaced by the individualism and the particularism of the bourgeoisie and of the popular classes.

The Fascist ideology cannot therefore look back to the Middle Ages, of which it is a complete negation. The Middle Ages spell disintegration; Fascism is nothing if not sociality. It is if anything the beginning of the end of the Middle Ages prolonged four centuries beyond the end ordinarily set for them and revived by the social democratic anarchy of the past thirty years. If Fascism can be said to look back at all it is rather in the direction of ancient Rome whose social and political traditions at the distance of fifteen centuries are being revived by Fascist Italy.

I am fully aware that the value of Fascism, as an intellectual movement, baffles the minds of many of its followers and supporters and is denied outright by its enemies. There is no malice in this denial, as I see it, but rather an incapacity to comprehend. The liberal-democratic-socialistic ideology has so completely and for so long a time dominated Italian culture that in the minds of the majority of people trained by it, it has assumed the value of an absolute truth, almost the authority of a natural law. Every faculty of self-criticism is suppressed in the minds and this suppression entails an incapacity for understanding that time alone can change. It will be advisable therefore to rely mainly upon the new generations and in general upon persons whose culture is not already fixed. This difficulty to comprehend on the part of those who have been thoroughly grounded by a different preparation in the political and social sciences explains in part why Fascism has not been wholly successful with the intellectual classes and with mature minds, and why on the other hand it has been very successful with young people, with women, in rural districts, and among men of action unencumbered by a fixed and set social and political education. Fascism moreover, as a cultural movement, is just now taking its first steps. As in the case with all great movements, action regularly outstrips thought. It was thus at the time of the Protestant Reformation and of the individualistic reaction of the 17th and 18th centuries. The English revolution occurred when the doctrines of natural law were coming into being and the theoretical development of the liberal and democratic theories followed the French Revolution.

At this point it will not be very difficult to assign a fitting place in history to this great trend of thought which is called Fascism and which, in spite of the initial difficulties, already gives clear indication of the magnitude of its developments.

The liberal-democratic speculation both in its origin and in the manner of its development appears to be essentially a non-Italian formation. Its connection with the Middle Ages already shows it to be foreign to the Latin mind, the mediaeval disintegration being the result of the triumph of Germanic individualism over the political mentality of the Romans. The barbarians, boring from within and hacking from without, pulled down the great political structure raised by Latin genius and put nothing in its place. Anarchy lasted eight centuries during which time only one institution survived and that a Roman one—the Catholic Church. But, as soon as the laborious process of reconstruction was started with the constitution of the great national states backed by the Roman Church the Protestant Reformation set in followed by the individualistic currents of the 17th and 18th centuries, and the process of disintegration was started anew. This anti-state tendency was the expression of the Germanic spirit and it therefore became predominant among the Germanic peoples and wherever Germanism had left a deep imprint even if afterward superficially covered by a veneer of Latin culture. It is true that Marsilius from Padua is an Italian writing for Ludwig the Bavarian, but the other writers who in the 14th century appear as forerunners of the liberal doctrines are not Italians: Occam and Wycliff are English; Oresme is French. Among the advocates of individualism in the 16th century who prepared the way for the triumph of the doctrines of natural law in the subsequent centuries, Hotman and Languet are French, Buchanan is Scotch. Of the great authorities of natural law, Grotius and Spinoza are Dutch; Locke is English; l'Abbé de St. Pierre, Montesquieu, d'Argenson, Voltaire, Rousseau, Diderot and the encyclopaedists are French; Althusius, Pufendorf, Kant, Fichte are German.

Italy took no part in the rise and development of the doctrines of natural law. Only in the 19th century did she evince a tardy interest in these doctrines, just as she tardily contributed to them at the close of the 18th century through the works of Beccaria and Filangeri.

While therefore in other countries such as France, England, Germany, and Holland, the general tradition in the social and political sciences worked in behalf of anti-state individualism, and therefore of liberal and democratic doctrines, Italy, on the other hand, clung to the powerful legacy of its past in virtue of which she proclaims the rights of the state, the preeminence of its authority, and the superiority of its ends. The very fact that the Italian political doctrine in the Middle Ages linked itself with the great political writers of antiquity, Plato and Aristotle, who in a different manner but with an equal firmness advocated a strong state and the subordination of individuals to it, is a sufficient index of the orientation of political philosophy in Italy. We all know how thorough and crushing the authority of Aristotle was in the Middle Ages. But for Aristotle the spiritual cement of the state is "virtue" not absolute virtue but political virtue, which is social devotion. His state is made up solely of its citizens, the citizens being either those who defend it with their arms or who govern it as magistrates. All others who provide it with the materials and services it needs are not citizens. They become such only in the corrupt forms of certain democracies. Society is therefore divided into two classes, the free men or citizens who give their time to noble and virtuous occupations and who profess their subjection to the state, and the laborers and slaves who work for the maintenance of the former. No man in this scheme is his own master. The slaves belong to the freemen, and the freemen belong to the state.

It was therefore natural that St. Thomas Aquinas the greatest political writer of the Middle Ages should emphasize the necessity of unity in the political field, the harm of plurality of rulers, the dangers and damaging effects of demagogy. The good of the state, says St. Thomas Aquinas, is unity. And who can procure unity more fittingly than he who is himself one? Moreover the government must follow, as far as possible, the course of nature and in nature power is always one. In the physical body only one organ is dominant—the heart; in the spirit only one faculty has sway—reason. Bees have one sole ruler; and the entire universe one sole sovereign—God. Experience shows that the countries, which are ruled by many, perish because of discord while those that are ruled over by one enjoy peace, justice, and plenty. The States which are not ruled by one are troubled by dissensions, and toil unceasingly. On the contrary the states which are ruled over by one king enjoy peace, thrive in justice and are gladdened by affluence. The rule of the multitudes can not be sanctioned, for where the crowd rules it oppresses the rich as would a tyrant.

Italy in the Middle Ages presented a curious phenomenon: while in practice the authority of the state was being dissolved into a multiplicity of competing sovereignties, the theory of state unity and authority was kept alive in the minds of thinkers by the memories of the Roman Imperial tradition. It was this memory that supported for centuries the fiction of the universal Roman Empire when in reality it existed no longer. Dante's De Monarchia deduced the theory of this empire conceived as the unity of a strong state. "*Quod potest fieri per unum melius est per unum fieri quam plura,*" he says in the 14th chapter of the first book, and further on, considering the citizen as an instrument for the attainment of the ends of the state, he concludes that the individual must sacrifice himself for his country. "*Si pars debet se exponere pro salute totius, cum homo siti pars quaedam civitatis ... homo pro patria debet exponere se ipsum.*" (lib. II. 8).

The Roman tradition, which was one of practice but not of theories— for Rome constructed the most solid state known to history with extraordinary statesmanship but with hardly any political writings— influenced considerably the founder of modern political science, Nicolo Machiavelli, who was himself in truth not a creator of doctrines but a keen observer of human nature who derived from the study of history practical maxims of political import. He freed the science of politics from the formalism of the scholastics and brought it close to concrete reality. His writings, an inexhaustible mine of practical remarks and precious observations, reveal dominant in him the state idea, no longer abstract but in the full historical concreteness of the national unity of Italy. Machiavelli therefore is not only the greatest of modern political writers, he is also the greatest of our countrymen in full possession of a national Italian consciousness. To liberate Italy, which was in his day "enslaved, torn and pillaged," and to make her more powerful, he would use any means, for to his mind the holiness of the end justified them completely. In this he was sharply rebuked by foreigners who were not as hostile to his means as they were fearful of the end which he propounded. He advocated therefore the constitution of a strong Italian state, supported by the sacrifices and by the blood of the citizens, not defended by mercenary troops; well-ordered internally, aggressive and bent on expansion. "Weak republics," he said, "have no determination and can never reach a decision." (Disc. I. c. 38). "Weak states were ever dubious in choosing their course, and slow deliberations are always harmful." (Disc. I. c. 10). And again: "Whoso undertakes to govern a multitude either in a régime of liberty or in a monarchy, without previously making sure of those who are hostile to the new order of things builds a short-lived state." (Disc. I. c. 16). And further on "the dictatorial authority helped and did not harm the Roman republic" (Disc. I. c. 34), and "Kings and republics lacking in national troops both for offense and defense should be ashamed of their existence." (Disc. I. c. 21). And again: "Money not only does not protect you but rather it exposes you to plundering assaults. Nor can there be a more false opinion than that which says that money is the sinews of war. Not money but good soldiers win battles." (Disc. I. II. c. 10). "The country must be defended with ignomy or with glory and in either way it is nobly defended." (Disc. III. c. 41). "And with dash and boldness people often capture what they never would have obtained by ordinary means." (Disc. III. c. 44). Machiavelli was not only a great political authority, he taught the mastery of energy and will. Fascism learns from him not only its doctrines but its action as well.

Different from Machiavelli's, in mental attitude, in cultural preparation, and in manner of presentation, G.B. Vico must yet be connected with the great Florentine from whom in a certain way he seems to proceed. In the heyday of "natural law" Vico is decidedly opposed to ius naturale and in his attacks against its advocates, Grotius, Seldenus and Pufendorf, he systematically assails the abstract, rationalistic, and utilitarian principles of the 18th century. As Montemayor justly says: "While the 'natural jurists', basing justice and state on utility and interest and grounding human certitude on reason, were striving to draft permanent codes and construct the perfect state, Vico strongly asserted the social nature of man, the ethical character of the juridical consciousness and its growth through the history of humanity rather than in sacred history. Vico therefore maintains that doctrines must begin with those subjects which take up and explain the entire course of civilization. Experience and not ratiocination, history and not reason must help human wisdom to understand the civil and political regimes which were the result not of reason or philosophy, but rather of common sense, or if you will of the social consciousness of man" and farther on (pages 373-374), "to Vico we owe the conception of history in its fullest sense as magistra vitae, the search after the humanity of history, the principle which makes the truth progress with time, the discovery of the political 'course' of nations. It is Vico who uttered the eulogy of the patrician 'heroic hearts' of the 'patres patriae' first founders of states, magnanimous defenders of the commonwealth and wise counsellors of politics. To Vico we owe the criticism of democracies, the affirmation of their brief existence, of their rapid disintegration at the hands of factions and demagogues, of their lapse first into anarchy, then into monarchy, when their degradation does not make them a prey of foreign oppressors. Vico conceived of civil liberty as subjection to law, as just subordination, of the private to the public interests, to the sway of the state. It was Vico who sketched modern society as a world of nations each one guarding its own imperium, fighting just and not inhuman wars. In Vico therefore we find the condemnation of pacifism, the assertion that right is actualized by bodily force, that without force, right is of no avail, and that therefore '*qui ab iniuriis se tueri non potest servus est.*'"

It is not difficult to discern the analogies between these affirmations and the fundamental views and the spirit of Fascism. Nor should we marvel at this similarity. Fascism, a strictly Italian phenomenon, has its roots in the Risorgimento and the Risorgimento was influenced undoubtedly by Vico.

It would be inexact to affirm that the philosophy of Vico dominated the Risorgimento. Too many elements of German, French, and English civilizations had been added to our culture during the first half of the 19th century to make this possible, so much so that perhaps Vico might have remained unknown to the makers of Italian unity if another powerful mind from Southern Italy, Vincenzo Cuoco, had not taken it upon himself to expound the philosophy of Vico in those very days in which the intellectual preparation of the Risorgimento was being carried on.

An adequate account of Cuoco's doctrines would carry me too far. Montemayor, in the article quoted above, gives them considerable attention. He quotes among other things Cuoco's arraignment of Democracy: "Italy has fared badly at the hand of Democracy which has withered to their roots the three sacred plants of liberty, unity, and independence. If we wish to see these trees flourish again let us protect them in the future from Democracy."

The influence of Cuoco, an exile at Milan, exerted through his writings, his newspaper articles, and Vichian propaganda, on the Italian patriots is universally recognized. Among the regular readers of his Giornale Italiano we find Monti and Foscolo. Clippings of his articles were treasured by Mazzini and Manzoni, who often acted as his secretary, called him his "master in politics."

The influence of the Italian tradition summed up and handed down by Cuoco was felt by Mazzini whose interpretation of the function of the citizen as duty and mission is to be connected with Vico's doctrine rather than with the philosophic and political doctrines of the French Revolution.

"Training for social duty," said Mazzini, "is essentially and logically unitarian. Life for it is but a duty, a mission. The norm and definition of such mission can only be found in a collective term superior to all the individuals of the country—in the people, in the nation. If there is a collective mission, a communion of duty ... it can only be represented in the national unity." And farther on: "The declaration of rights, which all constitutions insist in copying slavishly from the French, express only those of the period ... which considered the individual as the end and pointed out only one half of the problem" and again, "assume the existence of one of those crises that threaten the life of the nation, and demand the active sacrifice of all its sons ... will you ask the citizens to face martyrdom in virtue of their rights? You have taught men that society was solely constituted to guarantee their rights and now you ask them to sacrifice one and all, to suffer and die for the safety of the 'nation?'"

In Mazzini's conception of the citizen as instrument for the attainment of the nation's ends and therefore submissive to a higher mission, to the duty of supreme sacrifice, we see the anticipation of one of the fundamental points of the Fascist doctrine.

Unfortunately, the autonomy of the political thought of Italy, vigorously established in the works of Vico, nobly reclaimed by Vincenzo Cuoco, kept up during the struggles of the Risorgimento in spite of the many foreign influences of that period, seemed to exhaust itself immediately after the unification. Italian political thought which had been original in times of servitude, became enslaved in the days of freedom.

A powerful innovating movement, issuing from the war and of which Fascism is the purest expression, was to restore Italian thought in the sphere of political doctrine to its own traditions which are the traditions of Rome.

This task of intellectual liberation, now slowly being accomplished, is no less important than the political deliverance brought about by the Fascist Revolution. It is a great task which continues and integrates the Risorgimento; it is now bringing to an end, after the cessation of our political servitude, the intellectual dependence of Italy.

Thanks to it, Italy again speaks to the world and the world listens to Italy. It is a great task and a great deed and it demands great efforts. To carry it through, we must, each one of us, free ourselves of the dross of ideas and mental habits which two centuries of foreign intellectualistic tradition have heaped upon us; we must not only take on a new culture but create for ourselves a new soul. We must methodically and patiently contribute something towards the organic and complete elaboration of our doctrine, at the same time supporting it both at home and abroad with untiring devotion. We ask this effort of renovation and collaboration of all Fascists, as well as of all who feel themselves to be Italians. After the hour of sacrifice comes the hour of unyielding efforts. To our work, then, fellow countrymen, for the glory of Italy!

The Philosophic Basis of Fascism
by
Giovanni Gentile

Giovanni Gentile

The Philosophic Basis of Fascism

by Giovanni Gentile

For the Italian nation the World War was the solution of a deep spiritual crisis. They willed and fought it long before they felt and evaluated it. But they willed, fought, felt and evaluated it in a certain spirit which Italy's generals and statesmen exploited, but which also worked on them, conditioning their policies and their action. The spirit in question was not altogether clear and self-consistent. That it lacked unanimity was particularly apparent just before and again just after the war when feelings were not subject to war discipline. It was as though the Italian character were crossed by two different currents which divided it into two irreconcilable sections. One need think only of the days of Italian neutrality and of the debates that raged between Interventionists and Neutralists. The ease with which the most inconsistent ideas were pressed into service by both parties showed that the issue was not between two opposing political opinions, two conflicting concepts of history, but actually between two different temperaments, two different souls.

For one kind of person the important point was to fight the war, either on the side of Germany or against Germany: but in either event to fight the war, without regard to specific advantages—to fight the war in order that at last the Italian nation, created rather by favoring conditions than by the will of its people to be a nation, might receive its test in blood, such a test as only war can bring by uniting all citizens in a single thought, a single passion, a single hope, emphasizing to each individual that all have something in common, something transcending private interests.

This was the very thing that frightened the other kind of person, the prudent man, the realist, who had a clear view of the mortal risks a young, inexperienced, badly prepared nation would be running in such a war, and who also saw—a most significant point—that, all things considered, a bargaining neutrality would surely win the country tangible rewards, as great as victorious participation itself.

The point at issue was just that: the Italian Neutralists stood for material advantages, advantages tangible, ponderable, palpable; the Interventionists stood for moral advantages, intangible, impalpable, imponderable—imponderable at least on the scales used by their antagonists. On the eve of the war these two Italian characters

71

stood facing each other, scowling and irreconcilable—the one on the aggressive, asserting itself ever more forcefully through the various organs of public opinion; the other on the defensive, offering resistance through the Parliament which in those days still seemed to be the basic repository of State sovereignty. Civil conflict seemed inevitable in Italy, and civil war was in fact averted only because the King took advantage of one of his prerogatives and declared war against the Central Powers.

This act of the King was the first decisive step toward the solution of the crisis.

II

The crisis had ancient origins. Its roots sank deep into the inner spirit of the Italian people.

What were the creative forces of the Risorgimento? The "Italian people," to which some historians are now tending to attribute an important if not a decisive role in our struggle for national unity and independence, was hardly on the scene at all. The active agency was always an idea become a person—it was one or several determined wills which were fixed on determined goals. There can be no question that the birth of modern Italy was the work of the few. And it could not be otherwise. It is always the few who represent the self-consciousness and the will of an epoch and determine what its history shall be; for it is they who see the forces at their disposal and through those forces actuate the one truly active and productive force—their own will.

That will we find in the song of the poets and the ideas of the political writers, who know how to use a language harmonious with a universal sentiment or with a sentiment capable of becoming universal. In the case of Italy, in all our bards, philosophers and leaders, from Alfieri to Foscolo, from Leopardi to Manzoni, from Mazzini to Gioberti, we are able to pick up the threads of a new fabric, which is a new kind of thought, a new kind of soul, a new kind of Italy. This new Italy differed from the old Italy in something that was very simple but yet was of the greatest importance: this new Italy took life seriously, while the old one did not. People in every age had dreamed of an Italy and talked of an Italy. The notion of Italy had been sung in all kinds of music, propounded in all kinds of philosophy. But it was always an Italy that existed in the brain of some scholar whose learning was more or less divorced from reality. Now reality demands that convictions be taken seriously, that ideas become actions. Accordingly it was necessary that this Italy, which was an affair of brains only, become also an affair of hearts, become, that is, something serious, something alive. This, and no other, was the meaning of Mazzini's great slogan: "*Thought and Action.*" It was the essence of the great revolution which he preached and which he accomplished by instilling his doctrine into the hearts of others. Not many others—a small minority! But they were numerous enough and powerful enough to raise the question where it could be answered—in Italian public opinion (taken in conjunction with the political situation prevailing in the rest of Europe). They were able to establish the doctrine that life is not a game, but a mission; that, therefore, the individual has a law and a purpose in obedience to which and in fulfillment of which he alone attains his true value; that, accordingly, he must make sacrifices, now of personal comfort, now of private interest, now of life itself.

No revolution ever possessed more markedly than did the Italian Risorgimento this characteristic of ideality, of thought preceding action. Our revolt was not concerned with the material needs of life, nor did it spring from elementary and widely diffused sentiments breaking out in popular uprisings and mass disturbances. The movements of 1847 and 1848 were demonstrations, as we would say today, of "intellectuals"; they were efforts toward a goal on the part of a minority of patriots who were standard bearers of an ideal and were driving governments and peoples toward its attainment. Idealism— understood as faith in the advent of an ideal reality, as a manner of conceiving life not as fixed within the limits of existing fact, but as incessant progress and transformation toward the level of a higher law which controls men with the very force of the idea—was the sum and substance of Mazzini's teaching; and it supplied the most conspicuous characteristic of our great Italian revolution. In this sense all the patriots who worked for the foundation of the new kingdom were Mazzinians—Gioberti, Cavour, Victor Emmanuel, Garibaldi. To be sure, our writers of the first rank, such as Manzoni and Rosmini, had no historical connection with Mazzini; but they had the same general tendency as Mazzini. Working along diverging lines, they all came together on the essential point: that true life is not the life which is, but also the life which ought to be. It was a conviction essentially religious in character, essentially anti-materialistic.

III

This religious and idealistic manner of looking at life, so characteristic of the Risorgimento, prevails even beyond the heroic age of the revolution and the establishment of the Kingdom. It survives down through Ricasoli, Lanza, Sella and Minghetti, down, that is, to the occupation of Rome and the systemization of our national finances. The parliamentary overturn of 1876, indeed, marks not the end, but rather an interruption, on the road that Italy had been following since the beginning of the century. The outlook then changed, and not by the capriciousness or weakness of men, but by a necessity of history which it would be idiotic in our day to deplore. At that time the fall of the Right, which had ruled continuously between 1861 and 1876, seemed to most people the real conquest of freedom.

To be sure the Right cannot be accused of too great scruple in respecting the liberties guaranteed by our Constitution; but the real truth was that the Right conceived liberty in a sense directly opposite to the notions of the Left. The Left moved from the individual to the State: the Right moved from the State to the individual. The men of the left thought of "the people" as merely the agglomerate of the citizens composing it. They therefore made the individual the center and the point of departure of all the rights and prerogatives which a régime of freedom was bound to respect.

The men of the Right, on the contrary, were firmly set in the notion that no freedom can be conceived except within the State, that freedom can have no important content apart from a solid régime of law indisputably sovereign over the activities and the interests of individuals. For the Right there could be no individual freedom not reconcilable with the authority of the State. In their eyes the general interest was always paramount over private interests. The law, therefore, should have absolute efficacy and embrace the whole life of the people.

This conception of the Right was evidently sound; but it involved great dangers when applied without regard to the motives which provoked it. Unless we are careful, too much law leads to stasis and therefore to the annihilation of the life which it is the State's function to regulate but which the State cannot suppress. The State may easily become a form indifferent to its content—something extraneous to the substance it would regulate. If the law comes upon the individual from without, if the individual is not absorbed in the life of the State, the individual feels the law and the State as limitations on his activity, as chains which will eventually strangle him unless he can break them down.

This was just the feeling of the men of '76. The country needed a breath of air. Its moral, economic, and social forces demanded the right to develop without interference from a law which took no account of them. This was the historical reason for the overturn of that year; and with the transference of power from Right to Left begins the period of growth and development in our nation: economic growth in industry, commerce, railroads, agriculture; intellectual growth in science, education. The nation had received its form from above. It had now to struggle to its new level, giving to a State which already had its constitution, its administrative and political organization, its army and its finance, a living content of forces springing from individual initiative prompted by interests which the Risorgimento, absorbed in its great ideals, had either neglected or altogether disregarded.

The accomplishment of this constitutes the credit side of the balance sheet of King Humbert I. It was the error of King Humbert's greatest minister, Francesco Crispi, not to have understood his age. Crispi strove vigorously to restore the authority and the prestige of the State as against an individualism gone rampant, to reassert religious ideals as against triumphant materialism. He fell, therefore, before the assaults of so-called democracy.

Crispi was wrong. That was not the moment for re-hoisting the time-honored banner of idealism. At that time there could be no talk of wars, of national dignity, of competition with the Great Powers; no talk of setting limits to personal liberties in the interests of the abstract entity called "State." The word "God," which Crispi sometimes used, was singularly out of place. It was a question rather of bringing the popular classes to prosperity, self-consciousness, participation in political life. Campaigns against illiteracy, all kinds of social legislation, the elimination of the clergy from the public schools, which must be secular and anti-clerical! During this period Freemasonry became solidly established in the bureaucracy, the army, the judiciary. The central power of the State was weakened and made subservient to the fleeting variations of popular will as reflected in a suffrage absolved from all control from above. The growth of big industry favored the rise of a socialism of Marxian stamp as a new kind of moral and political education for our proletariat. The conception of humanity was not indeed lost from view: but such moral restraints as were placed on the free individual were all based on the feeling that each man must instinctively seek his own well-being and defend it. This was the very conception which Mazzini had fought in socialism, though he rightly saw that it was not peculiar to socialism alone, but belonged to any political theory, whether liberal, democratic, or anti-socialistic, which urges men toward the exaction of rights rather than to the fulfillment of duties.

From 1876 till the Great War, accordingly, we had an Italy that was materialistic and anti-Mazzinian, though an Italy far superior to the Italy of and before Mazzini's time. All our culture, whether in the natural or the moral sciences, in letters or in the arts, was dominated by a crude positivism, which conceived of the reality in which we live as something given, something ready-made, and which therefore limits and conditions human activity quite apart from so-called arbitrary and illusory demands of morality. Everybody wanted "facts," "positive facts." Everybody laughed at "metaphysical dreams," at impalpable realities. The truth was there before the eyes of men. They had only to open their eyes to see it. The Beautiful itself could only be the mirror of the Truth present before us in Nature. Patriotism, like all the other virtues based on a religious attitude of mind, and which can be mentioned only when people have the courage to talk in earnest, became a rhetorical theme on which it was rather bad taste to touch.

This period, which anyone born during the last half of the past century can well remember, might be called the demo-socialistic phase of the modern Italian State. It was the period which elaborated the characteristically democratic attitude of mind on a basis of personal freedom, and which resulted in the establishment of socialism as the primary and controlling force in the State. It was a period of growth and of prosperity during which the moral forces developed during the Risorgimento were crowded into the background or off the stage.

IV

But toward the end of the Nineteenth Century and in the first years of the Twentieth a vigorous spirit of reaction began to manifest itself in the young men of Italy against the preceding generation's ideas in politics, literature, science and philosophy. It was as though they were weary of the prosaic bourgeois life which they had inherited from their fathers and were eager to return to the lofty moral enthusiasms of their grandfathers. Rosmini and Gioberti had been long forgotten.

They were now exhumed, read, discussed. As for Mazzini, an edition of his writings was financed by the State itself. Vico, the great Vico, a formidable preacher of idealistic philosophy and a great anti-Cartesian and anti-rationalist, became the object of a new cult.

Positivism began forthwith to be attacked by neo-idealism. Materialistic approaches to the study of literature and art were refuted and discredited. Within the Church itself modernism came to rouse the Italian clergy to the need of a deeper and more modern culture. Even socialism was brought under the philosophical probe and criticized like other doctrines for its weaknesses and errors; and when, in France, George Sorel went beyond the fallacies of the materialistic theories of the Marxist social-democracy to his theory of syndicalism, our young Italian socialists turned to him. In Sorel's ideas they saw two things: first, the end of a hypocritical "collaborationism" which betrayed both proletariat and nation; and second, faith in a moral and ideal reality for which it was the individual's duty to sacrifice himself, and to defend which, even violence was justified. The anti-parliamentarian spirit and the moral spirit of syndicalism brought Italian socialists back within the Mazzinian orbit.

Of great importance, too, was nationalism, a new movement then just coming to the fore. Our Italian nationalism was less literary and more political in character than the similar movement in France, because with us it was attached to the old historic Right which had a long political tradition. The new nationalism differed from the old Right in the stress it laid on the idea of "nation"; but it was at one with the Right in regarding the State as the necessary premise to the individual rights and values. It was the special achievement of nationalism to rekindle faith in the nation in Italian hearts, to arouse the country against parliamentary socialism, and to lead an open attack on Freemasonry, before which the Italian bourgeoisie was terrifiedly prostrating itself. Syndicalists, nationalists, idealists succeeded, between them, in bringing the great majority of Italian youth back to the spirit of Mazzini.

Official, legal, parliamentary Italy, the Italy that was anti-Mazzinian and anti-idealistic, stood against all this, finding its leader in a man of unfailing political intuition, and master as well of the political mechanism of the country, a man sceptical of all high-sounding words, impatient of complicated concepts, ironical, cold, hard-headed, practical—what Mazzini would have called a "shrewd materialist." In the persons, indeed, of Mazzini and Giolitti, we may find a picture of the two aspects of pre-war Italy, of that irreconcilable duality which paralyzed the vitality of the country and which the Great War was to solve.

V

The effect of the war seemed at first to be quite in an opposite sense—to mark the beginning of a general débâcle of the Italian State and of the moral forces that must underlie any State. If entrance into the war had been a triumph of ideal Italy over materialistic Italy, the advent of peace seemed to give ample justification to the Neutralists who had represented the latter. After the Armistice our Allies turned their backs upon us. Our victory assumed all the aspects of a defeat. A defeatist psychology, as they say, took possession of the Italian people and expressed itself in hatred of the war, of those responsible for the war, even of our army which had won our war. An anarchical spirit of dissolution rose against all authority. The ganglia of our economic life seemed struck with mortal disease. Labor ran riot in strike after strike. The very bureaucracy seemed to align itself against the State. The measure of our spiritual dispersion was the return to power of Giolitti—the execrated Neutralist—who for five years had been held up as the exponent of an Italy which had died with the war.

But, curiously enough, it was under Giolitti that things suddenly changed in aspect, that against the Giolittian State a new State arose. Our soldiers, our genuine soldiers, men who had willed our war and fought it in full consciousness of what they were doing, had the good fortune to find as their leaders a man who could express in words things that were in all their hearts and who could make those words audible above the tumult.

Mussolini had left Italian socialism in 1915 in order to be a more faithful interpreter of "the Italian People" (the name he chose for his new paper). He was one of those who saw the necessity of our war, one of those mainly responsible for our entering the war. Already as a socialist he had fought Freemasonry; and, drawing his inspiration from Sorel's syndicalism, he had assailed the parliamentary corruption of Reformist Socialism with the idealistic postulates of revolution and violence. Then, later, on leaving the party and in defending the cause of intervention, he had come to oppose the illusory fancies of proletarian internationalism with an assertion of the infrangible integrity, not only moral but economic as well, of the national organism, affirming therefore the sanctity of country for the working classes as for other classes. Mussolini was a Mazzinian of that pure-blooded breed which Mazzini seemed somehow always to find in the province of Romagna. First by instinct, later by reflection, Mussolini had come to despise the futility of the socialists who kept preaching a revolution which they had neither the power nor the will to bring to pass even under the most favorable circumstances. More keenly than anyone else he had come to feel the necessity of a State which would be a State, of a law which would be respected as law, of an authority capable of exacting obedience but at the same time able to give indisputable evidence of its worthiness so to act. It seemed incredible to Mussolini that a country capable of fighting and winning such a war as Italy had fought and won should be thrown into disorder and held at the mercy of a handful of faithless politicians.

When Mussolini founded his Fasci in Milan in March, 1919, the movement toward dissolution and negation that featured the post-war period in Italy had virtually ceased. The Fasci made their appeal to Italians who, in spite of the disappointments of the peace, continued to believe in the war, and who, in order to validate the victory which was the proof of the war's value, were bent on recovering for Italy that control over her own destinies which could come only through a restoration of discipline and a reorganization of social and political forces. From the first, the Fascist Party was not one of believers but of action. What it needed was not a platform of principles, but an idea which would indicate a goal and a road by which the goal could be reached.

The four years between 1919 and 1923 inclusive were characterized by the development of the Fascist revolution through the action of "the squads." The Fascist "squads" were really the force of a State not yet born but on the way to being. In its first period, Fascist "squadrism" transgressed the law of the old régime because it was determined to suppress that régime as incompatible with the national State to which Fascism was aspiring. The March on Rome was not the beginning, it was the end of that phase of the revolution; because, with Mussolini's advent to power, Fascism entered the sphere of legality. After October 28, 1922, Fascism was no longer at war with the State; it was the State, looking about for the organization which would realize Fascism as a concept of State. Fascism already had control of all the instruments necessary for the upbuilding of a new State. The Italy of Giolitti had been superceded, at least so far as militant politics were concerned. Between Giolitti's Italy and the new Italy there flowed, as an imaginative orator once said in the Chamber, "a torrent of blood" that would prevent any return to the past. The century-old crisis had been solved. The war at last had begun to bear fruit for Italy.

VI

Now to understand the distinctive essence of Fascism, nothing is more instructive than a comparison of it with the point of view of Mazzini to which I have so often referred.

Mazzini did have a political conception, but his politic was a sort of integral politic, which cannot be so sharply distinguished from morals, religion, and ideas of life as a whole, as to be considered apart from these other fundamental interests of the human spirit. If one tries to separate what is purely political from his religious beliefs, his ethical consciousness and his metaphysical concepts, it becomes impossible to understand the vast influence which his credo and his propaganda exerted. Unless we assume the unity of the whole man, we arrive not at the clarification but at the destruction of those ideas of his which proved so powerful.

In the definition of Fascism, the first point to grasp is the comprehensive, or as Fascists say, the "totalitarian" scope of its doctrine, which concerns itself not only with political organization and political tendency, but with the whole will and thought and feeling of the nation.

There is a second and equally important point. Fascism is not a philosophy. Much less is it a religion. It is not even a political theory which may be stated in a series of formulae. The significance of Fascism is not to be grasped in the special theses which it from time to time assumes. When on occasion it has announced a program, a goal, a concept to be realized in action, Fascism has not hesitated to abandon them when in practice these were found to be inadequate or inconsistent with the principle of Fascism. Fascism has never been willing to compromise its future. Mussolini has boasted that he is a tempista, that his real pride is in "good timing." He makes decisions and acts on them at the precise moment when all the conditions and considerations which make them feasible and opportune are properly matured. This is a way of saying that Fascism returns to the most rigorous meaning of Mazzini's "Thought and Action," whereby the two terms are so perfectly coincident that no thought has value which is not already expressed in action. The real "views" of the Duce are those which he formulates and executes at one and the same time.

The Philosophic Basis of Fascism

Is Fascism therefore "anti-intellectual," as has been so often charged? It is eminently anti-intellectual, eminently Mazzinian, that is, if by intellectualism we mean the divorce of thought from action, of knowledge from life, of brain from heart, of theory from practice. Fascism is hostile to all Utopian systems which are destined never to face the test of reality. It is hostile to all science and all philosophy which remain matters of mere fancy or intelligence. It is not that Fascism denies value to culture, to the higher intellectual pursuits by which thought is invigorated as a source of action. Fascist anti-intellectualism holds in scorn a product peculiarly typical of the educated classes in Italy: the *leterato*—the man who plays with knowledge and with thought without any sense of responsibility for the practical world. It is hostile not so much to culture as to bad culture, the culture which does not educate, which does not make men, but rather creates pedants and aesthetes, egotists in a word, men morally and politically indifferent. It has no use, for instance, for the man who is "above the conflict" when his country or its important interests are at stake.

By virtue of its repugnance for "intellectualism," Fascism prefers not to waste time constructing abstract theories about itself. But when we say that it is not a system or a doctrine we must not conclude that it is a blind praxis or a purely instinctive method. If by system or philosophy we mean a living thought, a principle of universal character daily revealing its inner fertility and significance, then Fascism is a perfect system, with a solidly established foundation and with a rigorous logic in its development; and all who feel the truth and the vitality of the principle work day by day for its development, now doing, now undoing, now going forward, now retracing their steps, according as the things they do prove to be in harmony with the principle or to deviate from it.

The Fascist system is not a political system, but it has its center of gravity in politics. Fascism came into being to meet serious problems of politics in post-war Italy. And it presents itself as a political method. But in confronting and solving political problems it is carried by its very nature, that is to say by its method, to consider moral, religious, and philosophical questions and to unfold and demonstrate the comprehensive totalitarian character peculiar to it. It is only after we have grasped the political character of the Fascist principle that we are able adequately to appreciate the deeper concept of life which underlies that principle and from which the principle springs. The political doctrine of Fascism is not the whole of Fascism. It is rather its more prominent aspect and in general its most interesting one.

VII

The politic of Fascism revolves wholly about the concept of the national State; and accordingly it has points of contact with nationalist doctrines, along with distinctions from the latter which it is important to bear in mind.

Both Fascism and nationalism regard the State as the foundation of all rights and the source of all values in the individuals composing it. For the one as for the other the State is not a consequence—it is a principle. But in the case of nationalism, the relation which individualistic liberalism, and for that matter socialism also, assumed between individual and State is inverted. Since the State is a principle, the individual becomes a consequence—he is something which finds an antecedent in the State: the State limits him and determines his manner of existence, restricting his freedom, binding him to a piece of ground whereon he was born, whereon he must live and will die. In the case of Fascism, State and individual are one and the same things, or rather, they are inseparable terms of a necessary synthesis.

Nationalism, in fact, founds the State on the concept of nation, the nation being an entity which transcends the will and the life of the individual because it is conceived as objectively existing apart from the consciousness of individuals, existing even if the individual does nothing to bring it into being. For the nationalist, the nation exists not by virtue of the citizen's will, but as datum, a fact, of nature.

For Fascism, on the contrary, the State is a wholly spiritual creation. It is a national State, because, from the Fascist point of view, the nation itself is a creation of the mind and is not a material presupposition, is not a datum of nature. The nation, says the Fascist, is never really made; neither, therefore, can the State attain an absolute form, since it is merely the nation in the latter's concrete, political manifestation. For the Fascist, the State is always in fieri. It is in our hands, wholly; whence our very serious responsibility towards it.

But this State of the Fascists which is created by the consciousness and the will of the citizen, and is not a force descending on the citizen from above or from without, cannot have toward the mass of the population the relationship which was presumed by nationalism.

Nationalism identified State with Nation, and made of the nation an entity preexisting, which needed not to be created but merely to be recognized or known. The nationalists, therefore, required a ruling class of an intellectual character, which was conscious of the nation and could understand, appreciate and exalt it. The authority of the State, furthermore, was not a product but a presupposition. It could not depend on the people—rather the people depended on the State and on the State's authority as the source of the life which they lived and apart from which they could not live. The nationalistic State was, therefore, an aristocratic State, enforcing itself upon the masses through the power conferred upon it by its origins.

The Fascist State, on the contrary, is a people's state, and, as such, the democratic State par excellence. The relationship between State and citizen (not this or that citizen, but all citizens) is accordingly so intimate that the State exists only as, and in so far as, the citizen causes it to exist. Its formation therefore is the formation of a consciousness of it in individuals, in the masses. Hence the need of the Party, and of all the instruments of propaganda and education which Fascism uses to make the thought and will of the Duce the thought and will of the masses. Hence the enormous task which Fascism sets itself in trying to bring the whole mass of the people, beginning with the little children, inside the fold of the Party.

On the popular character of the Fascist State likewise depends its greatest social and constitutional reform—the foundation of the Corporations of Syndicates. In this reform Fascism took over from syndicalism the notion of the moral and educational function of the syndicate. But the Corporations of Syndicates were necessary in order to reduce the syndicates to State discipline and make them an expression of the State's organism from within. The Corporation of Syndicates are a device through which the Fascist State goes looking for the individual in order to create itself through the individual's will. But the individual it seeks is not the abstract political individual whom the old liberalism took for granted. He is the only individual who can ever be found, the individual who exists as a specialized productive force, and who, by the fact of his specialization, is brought to unite with other individuals of his same category and comes to belong with them to the one great economic unit which is none other than the nation.

This great reform is already well under way. Toward it nationalism, syndicalism, and even liberalism itself, were already tending in the past. For even liberalism was beginning to criticize the older forms of political representation, seeking some system of organic representation which would correspond to the structural reality of the State.

The Fascist conception of liberty merits passing notice. The Duce of Fascism once chose to discuss the theme of "Force or consent?"; and he concluded that the two terms are inseparable, that the one implies the other and cannot exist apart from the other; that, in other words, the authority of the State and the freedom of the citizen constitute a continuous circle wherein authority presupposes liberty and liberty authority. For freedom can exist only within the State, and the State means authority. But the State is not an entity hovering in the air over the heads of its citizens. It is one with the personality of the citizen. Fascism, indeed, envisages the contrast not as between liberty and authority, but as between a true, a concrete liberty which exists, and an abstract, illusory liberty which cannot exist.

Liberalism broke the circle above referred to, setting the individual against the State and liberty against authority. What the liberal desired was liberty as against the State, a liberty which was a limitation of the State; though the liberal had to resign himself, as the lesser of the evils, to a State which was a limitation on liberty. The absurdities inherent in the liberal concept of freedom were apparent to liberals themselves early in the Nineteenth Century. It is no merit of Fascism to have again indicated them. Fascism has its own solution of the paradox of liberty and authority. The authority of the State is absolute. It does not compromise, it does not bargain, it does not surrender any portion of its field to other moral or religious principles which may interfere with the individual conscience. But on the other hand, the State becomes a reality only in the consciousness of its individuals. And the Fascist corporative State supplies a representative system more sincere and more in touch with realities than any other previously devised and is therefore freer than the old liberal State.

Lightning Source UK Ltd.
Milton Keynes UK
UKHW051710160719
346204UK00018B/220/P